Mystery of Memory

Telling My Truth, Standing My Ground

"The greater the doubt, the greater the awakening;
The smaller the doubt, the smaller the awakening;
No doubt, no awakening."

C. Chang, *The Practice of Zen*

by **Deborah Howard**

guiding change

© 2017 Deborah Howard

All rights reserved. No part of this publication may be reproduced or transmitted in any form or by any means electronic or mechanical, including photocopy, recording, or any information storage and retrieval system, without permission in writing from the copyright owner.

ISBN: 978-1-62550-505-7 (PB)
  978-1-62550-506-4 (EB)

Acknowledgments

I would like to express my love and gratitude to the following people who helped me in unique and essential ways. I could never have finished this journey without them.

Cullen Thomas for telling me that this was the story I needed to write and helping me start writing it. Aeric Meredith-Goujon who helped me better tell my story.

Yvette Hyater-Adams for talking me through many tough times, Laura Kelber for believing me from the start, Tony Bennae Richard for always being there and Yvonne Shinhoster-Lamb for saying what I needed to hear when I needed to hear it.

Bart Crawford, Linda Faigo-Hall, Julian Griggs, Denise Harding, Chaumtoli Huq, Laura Kelber, Edwina Mendelson, Antonia Marrero, and Maise Rubenstein, who reviewed and commented on drafts and provided moral support along the way.

Author's Note

This is my memoir. It is my story as I recall it. All characters are real although I changed the names of some to respect their privacy. Whenever possible, I used letters, diaries, newspaper articles and interviews with others to confirm dates and events. I have done my best to capture conversations and while every word may not be exact, the essence of each conversation is as accurate as possible.

It is my hope that this book will empower others (particularly those who have been marginalized and silenced) to speak out, stand their ground and be heard.

Table of Contents

I.	**My Vision**	1
	Depression	3
	Family Photos	8
	Hypnosis	13
	Parents Like Mine	16
	What Else I Know About My Parents	22
	Some Childhood Memories	27
II.	**The Confrontation**	31
	I Move to Alaska	31
	Feelings Begin to Surface	33
	Shame and Other Sensations	36
	The Confrontation	39
	The Acknowledgement	50
	I Move to Japan	55
III.	**Incest & Insanity**	57
	NUTS	57
	I Hit A Wall: My Father Recants	66
	I Begin to Question My Reality	71
	I Reach Out Again	73
	More Invisibility	78
	A Meeting is Brokered	82
IV.	**I Rest My Case**	84
	Mother's Day	84
	My Supreme Court Brief	85
	My Marriage	87
	Reconciliation and Acceptance	90
	I Share a Piece of My Story	94

	I Find Peace	101
V.	**SELF DOUBT AND DISCOVERY**	**105**
	My Parents Pass Away	**105**
	I Decide to Confront My Self-Doubt Head On	106
	I Become a Detective	108
	I Learn More About My Parents	119
VI.	**TELLING MY TRUTH, STANDING MY GROUND**	**127**
	I Talk with My Brother	127
	The "Great Incest War"	136
	My Body Tells the Story	140
	From Forgiveness to Empathy	142
	Telling My Truth, Standing My Ground	145

Mystery of Memory

Telling My Truth, Standing My Ground

I. My Vision

I lay on my bed. My mind felt like it was expanding; I no longer felt present in my body. I was dreaming. I was awake. I saw an empty stage, a closed black curtain. In front of the curtain, me, as a young girl of twelve. From deep inside her chest, a stream of tears, spewing like a fountain. Years' worth pouring out, unstoppable. She asks, "Are you sure you want to know this?"

"This" means the source of my depression and the deep well of grief flowing from her chest.

I remembered psychology class, "catharsis." Emotional release from recalling repressed trauma.

I want relief from the depression that leaves me stranded in bed every morning.

This must be the only way.

I answer, "Yes."

My twelve-year old self responds, "Daddy raped me."

***

This vision came to me in the winter of 1980. I was a pale, five-foot-two, second-year law student in my early twenties at Northeastern University. I lived in a mouse-infested apartment on the second floor of a small house in the Jamaica Plain section of Boston. That summer, I'd started dating Miguel, a fellow law student. He was a light-skinned Puerto Rican man with curly black hair, glasses, and a scruffy beard. He wanted to be a public defender. I loved eating the food he prepared:

vegetarian lasagna, soup with corn and potatoes, sandwiches on wheat bread with alfalfa sprouts. He called me "New York-New York" because of my constant motion, my hyper energy, and how fast I walked. He also called me his *tigre* because I had a black belt in judo and could pull him off balance unexpectedly by sweeping one of his feet out from under him. Maybe also because I refused to bring the four-inch thick Civil Procedure textbook to class, knowing my professor would give me the evil eye whenever he asked us to open our books and mine was never there.

On New Year's Eve, Miguel, and our two friends Paul and Cecilia, came to my apartment to celebrate. Paul, like Miguel, was a law school classmate. We knew each other well, but I only knew Cecilia through Paul. The evening started uneventfully. The four of us sat in my living room drinking wine and cheap Champagne. Paul lit a joint and offered it around. This was probably the second or third time I'd ever smoked marijuana; I tried to keep from coughing and making my inexperience obvious. Without knowing why, I felt myself becoming distant, like I was slipping away from the others, and before midnight came around, I was crying softly. Miguel couldn't see the tears, but sitting across from me, Paul did. He knelt in front of me and lifted my face with his hands. "Deb, look at me, what's the matter?"

Unable to answer, I kept my eyes down and shook my head.

"Did something happen?" Miguel asked. He joined Paul on the floor in front of me.

The more they tried to console me, the heavier the tears, the more I wanted to be invisible. I heard the others talking to me, but as if in a state of shock, I was unable to speak or stop crying.

Miguel pulled Paul and Cecilia aside and whispered, "I think maybe you guys should leave."

"All right, but do you think she's gonna be OK?" asked Paul.

"I think right now she just needs some space. I'll be with her."

After they left, Miguel guided me to my bedroom, his arm around my shoulders, and helped me lie down. I was still sobbing. The mattress shifted as he lay down beside me, his hands stroking my face as I closed my eyes. Increasingly agitated, Miguel asked, "Deb, what's the matter? What happened? What can I do? Are you OK?"

Sensing his alarm and worry, I wished I could allay his fears, but I still wasn't able to speak and couldn't explain what was happening to me even if I could. Slowly, my crying subsided. I was aware of where I was and that Miguel was there in the room with me. I knew I was lying on my bed on top of the Mexican blanket with an eagle that I'd used for a bedspread since I was in high school.

Then my vision came.

I'd never had an experience like that before. I don't believe it was related to the marijuana; as soon as the vision ended, I came fully back into my body and the room. I was neither foggy-headed nor high. I opened my eyes, looked at Miguel and told him what happened. His eyes opened wide as he took in my words.

Depression

My relationship with Miguel was idyllic. An active runner, he convinced me to start running regularly with him. We ran around the tree-lined pond in Jamaica Plain in the early morning. I enjoyed seeing the green trees and hearing the crunch of gravel under our feet. On weekends, when we had more time, we ran along the Charles River, back and forth across the various bridges between Boston and Cambridge. Miguel taught me how to drive a stick shift in his orange VW. Enclosed in this orange ladybug-like shell of a car, he sat in the driver's seat, steering and operating the clutch. I sat in the passenger seat with my body stretched all the way left, changing the gears with my right arm.

Less than six months after I started dating Miguel, I had difficulty getting up in the morning. For no clear reason, I was weepy and experiencing a sense of hopelessness. I curled into myself, in bed or on the couch in the living room. I had no interest in doing anything or going anywhere. I was consumed with feelings of worthlessness and self-hatred, unlike anything I had experienced before. I felt like I had suddenly fallen into a pit and was stuck, unable to climb out.

Miguel would call, "C'mon Deb, let's go running this morning,"

"I don't feel like it. I just wanna be alone today."

If absolutely necessary, I functioned, but it was like moving through heavy, thick mud. When I had to interview for an internship position I had applied for weeks before, I pulled on pantyhose and selected a suitable skirt and blouse. During the interview, I marshaled just enough energy to be able to turn my lips up into a smile, raising my cheekbones: my equivalent of a "game face."

Since high school, I'd experienced bouts of sadness between my relationships with men, but this was different. I was weighed down and lethargic. I had no energy to be active and not even the things I loved felt pleasurable. The depth of this depression was new to me and I couldn't understand why I would be feeling this way when I was in a secure, loving relationship.

***

When my depression persisted for more than two weeks, Miguel got the name of a therapist from a friend. I went to see Pierre on a winter afternoon in late December. The office was simply furnished with a large desk and two chairs. I saw the darkening sky outside the window behind Pierre, a slightly overweight black man.

He looked at me over his steel-rimmed glasses. "So, tell me why you're here."

"I don't know. I've been depressed for a few weeks."

"Why do you think you're depressed?"

Before I was able to say a word, I broke down crying. I hunched forward in the chair, hands over my eyes, unable to look at Pierre. In the space between sobs, I told him, "I don't know why... I don't remember anything bad happening to me."

"Tell me a little about your family."

"I have a normal family."

"Tell me about them."

Mystery of Memory

"I don't know what to tell you."

"Well, what do your parents do for a living?"

"My father's a Vice President at a Madison Avenue advertising agency. He's been with them for years. My mother's a senior administrator for the New York City Department of the Aging. She's been doing that for a while. Before that, she did something for the Board of Education. I don't remember her being home when I was little but she told me she worked only part-time during the first few years I was in elementary school."

"Do you have any siblings?"

"Yes, a brother—he's two years older than me."

"Anything else you can tell me about your family?"

"Well, everyone's tall except me. My father and brother are almost six feet tall and my mother is five-foot-eight. I think I may have stunted my growth because I was a vegetarian for about a year when I was in the sixth grade. But my mother's mother was short so maybe I took after her."

"What are your parents like?"

"Well, we're Jewish but you wouldn't think that about my mother. She seems more like a WASP. She doesn't show much emotion—I can count on half of one hand the number of times I've seen her cry."

"What about your father?"

"Oh, he gets emotional all the time. He gets teary-eyed in a minute—he cries when he watches a sappy commercial. He's hyper and doesn't know how to relax. He can't stroll or walk slowly. He walks fast, leaning forward as if that'll help him get where he's going faster. Even if the family's watching TV, if he wants to get a snack during a commercial, he marches into the kitchen as if he's on an important mission."

"What can you tell me about your childhood?"

"I'm not sure."

"Just tell me whatever comes to mind."

I leaned back, sensing the hard wood of the chair-back supporting me, and closed my eyes. I could see pictures. But they weren't memories. They were actual snapshots from family photo albums: me alone standing by the water at a beach; me with my brother playing in the sand; my brother, my parents and me sitting under a beach umbrella.

At the time, and for many years after, I was under the impression that I had almost no childhood memories, certainly none that could explain my depression or the vision. But it's clear to me now, in writing this book, that I do have memories from my childhood. Perhaps I thought that "memories" consisted of movie-like scenes, seeing action and hearing conversation. I wasn't able to retrieve anything like that. One reason I may not have many of those kinds of memories is there wasn't much in the way of storytelling in my family. There were only a few times either of my parents talked about their youth or retold stories about my brother's and my childhood.

***

Why had I suddenly dropped into and gotten stuck in a pit of depression? I had no idea. But shortly after my first meeting with Pierre, I experienced that vision on New Year's Eve. It felt like a puzzle piece had slid into place.

When I woke up New Year's Day, the weight of the depression had lifted. I experienced a sense of lightness and clarity, and felt purified, as if a shameful burden had been taken off my shoulders.

The worthlessness and self-hatred were gone. I had a sensation of emotional liberation. Weirdly, I experienced a physical cleansing as well. My face, which until that morning had been riddled with acne, had completely cleared up overnight.

Sitting at the small table in my eat-in kitchen with Miguel, we talked about what happened the night before. We agreed it was no coincidence that my face cleared up and my depression had lifted.

***

The vision provided an explanation for the depression. I felt such immense relief that it didn't occur to me there would be any consequences to this discovery. I felt no anger or sadness, only relief.

Mystery of Memory

I was anxious to see Pierre for the second time. I felt I'd solved the problem of my depression. I had no idea that I'd experience any feelings other than continued relief. I was curious, however, about what actually happened between my father and me.

Sitting across from Pierre, I told him what happened. This time, I didn't cry.

"So, if my father raped me, how is it possible that I don't have any memories of that happening?"

Pierre's chair squeaked as he tilted it back. He let out a sigh. "Well, it's possible you have repressed memories of your father sexually abusing you. But it's too soon to know for sure. Your vision may be a 'screen'—an image covering up something else." Leaning forward, he went on, "Let's see what we can figure out. Have you been able to remember anything else about your childhood since we first met?"

"No, all I can see in my head are pictures from the family photo albums."

"Well, maybe if you look at them, it might help you come up with some memories. Can you have your parents send you these albums?"

***

My father answered the phone. Despite the traumatic nature of my vision, I wasn't in touch with any emotions other than relief and curiosity. The only discomfort I experienced talking to my father was a little apprehension about asking him to send me the photo albums.

I imagined him sitting at his desk in the "study," the small room off of my parents' bedroom. A long wooden plank mounted on the wall with a small bureau underneath served as a desk for both my parents. His side was near the window and hers was against the opposite wall. His hair, about an inch long, had been salt and pepper (mainly salt) as long as I could remember. I explained that I had started therapy for depression, but since I couldn't remember much about my childhood, my therapist had asked me to look over the albums to see if they might spark some memories. I heard him take a breath, followed by a long exhale.

"Deborah, these are the only copies we have of these photos. Is it really necessary for us to send them? I don't want them to get lost or damaged." I imagined him sitting up straight as he spoke, his forehead furrowed and his right eyebrow raised under his sharp widow's peak.

I recalled incidents involving that eyebrow. The good ones were of my father teaching my older brother Aaron and me how to raise one eyebrow when I was about ten years old. I was quite proud when I finally learned to do it. The bad memories are of my father's angry face. I remember him standing in front of the three steps in the dining room leading to the outdoor deck. I don't remember why he was angry, but when his right eyebrow rose above his piercing glare, my body stiffened and my breath got shallow.

While we were on the phone, his voice was inquiring and higher-pitched. I was surprised when he gave in to my request. A few days later, I went to the bus station in Boston. I guess it was cheaper at the time to send the albums by bus than by UPS or Fed Ex. They were packed in an old black suitcase made out of a cardboard-like material, but stronger. My father, a master packer, had surrounded the albums in the suitcase with crumpled newspaper to keep them from shifting.

The albums had black covers with orange pages, on which the photos were all glued into place. Seeing them reminded me of my childhood best friend Laura and I pulling them out when we were bored. We'd sit next to each other on the honey-colored couch in the living room at my home in Brooklyn. We loved looking at all the pictures of family and friends, some from before my brother and I were born. The albums we'd pored over for fun were the same ones I brought to my next therapy session.

FAMILY PHOTOS

The photo albums my father sent ranged from when I was an infant through my high school years. All the photos were familiar since Laura and I had looked at them so many times. I recognized all the images, but I wasn't able to come up with memories of the actual experiences

MYSTERY OF MEMORY

they represented. I could recall general events not recorded in the albums—playing stoopball, hide-and-go-seek, or tag outside with neighbors on our block; sitting at the table for dinner when my father told my brother and me, "Children should be seen and not heard." Almost all my recollections were of static images and few were of specific conversations or interactions. None of them gave me any clues about the meaning of my vision.

***

In writing this book, I looked over the same photo albums to see what they would evoke. There's a photo of my brother and me playing in the park with my father. I was four and Aaron was six. My father is on all fours and I'm sitting on his back like I'm riding a horse. Aaron has a fistful of my father's shirt in his right hand while trying to boost himself up by pushing against the back of my father's neck with his other hand. I have no memories of my brother and I playing with my father in the park that day or any other.

When my brother and I were both a little older, we played what my father called "roughhouse." He was usually on the living room floor on his hands and knees and we'd tackle him. I can feel the carpet, scratchy against my knees as my brother and I pounced on the seemingly unassailable firmness of my father's back. My brother tried to hit him once, and my father told us he would hit back: "One for one."

I have a memory of swimming with my father, during a family vacation when we stayed someplace that had a small round swimming pool about six feet deep surrounded by a concrete patio. I was about four years old and didn't know how to swim, but I loved the water. I hung onto the side of the pool until my father had me hold onto his shoulders as he swam around. Gliding through the water with his broad shoulders underneath me keeping me above water, was wonderful.

My father swam fairly well, but my mother was a skillful swimmer. While I never thought of her as athletic—as a skier, she was always tense and stiff, and I never saw her run—as a swimmer, she was different. I have a vivid memory of her in a black swimsuit swimming laps with long, even, strong strokes moving her across the length of a pool and back.

In one of the many beach photos in the albums, my brother and I are playing in the sand. Squatting and leaning forward with sand-covered hands, he's smoothing out an area in front of me. He's wearing a dark blue bathing suit and a blue swimming mask pushed up on his forehead, with a yellow snorkel attached. I'm on the right, sitting with my knees bent and my elbows touching the insides of my legs, my hands on each side of the spot where my brother is patting down the sand. I'm looking down at what he's doing. My hair is about shoulder length but the hair on top is tied up with a rubber band.

I don't remember playing with my brother on the beach that day or my mother putting my hair up in that tiny ponytail. But looking at that picture brought to mind a time my mother took me to get my bangs cut. "Your bangs are so long, you can't even see."

I was mad because she had the barber cut them about two inches above my eyes. They seemed ridiculously short to me and made my forehead look enormous.

That reminded me of the only memory I have of my mother touching my hair. I was older, maybe eight or nine, with longer hair and no bangs. My mother brushed the hair back off my forehead and held it in place with a headband. "Your hair looks so nice off your face like this. And if you don't wear it this way, you'll have a permanent part in your hair." I hated the way it looked. I wanted my hair down, covering my forehead.

There are a few pictures taken during a family trip to Nantucket when I was six. To get to the beach from the house we stayed in, you had to go down a long stairway with one hundred steps. I know because we counted them.

My Aunt Joan, my mother's younger sister, was with us that summer. My brother and I loved her. We saw her as different from other adults because she cursed like a sailor and had us call her "Joan," not "Aunt Joan." She was usually fun to be with but this occasion was an exception. My brother and I took a walk through the reeds and grass along the side of the house. We went exploring; I followed his lead. When we were done, we came back excited and tired. "Where did you go?" asked Joan.

When we told her, she was furious. "There's poison ivy out there and you probably have it all over you! Take off your clothes right now and get in the tub." She acted as if we'd committed a crime. She scrubbed us with Lava soap. It felt as if it would go on forever; my skin felt raw by the time she was done.

In another photo, I'm sitting on a white horse that my father is leading by the reins. As with the beach house with the one hundred steps, I remember riding this horse. We were in Cornell, New York, staying with Gladys, an old friend of my parents, on her farm. I was about six years old and recall how huge the horse seemed to me. In the picture, I'm sitting up straight on the saddle with my feet in the stirrups. My hair is pushed back off my forehead with a headband and I'm looking at the camera with my mouth closed and lips relaxed.

Another thing I remember about Cornell was fishing with my brother in the nearby pond. Neither of us had ever fished before. Gladys made us makeshift fishing poles with some long branches and pieces of string. She tied one end of the string to the narrow part of each branch and attached hooks to the other end. Then we put worms on the hooks. We stood at the edge of the pond casting our lines of string out as far as we could. I caught a fish and Aaron didn't. I was delighted because usually he was the one who could do things I wasn't able to do.

There are two photos of me at home in Brooklyn on my sixth birthday, holding a stuffed animal. I don't remember anything about that day, or the birthday party I must have had, but have a vivid memory of that stuffed animal. It was a black cat with fur so real that touching it was like petting a live cat. I got two of those on that birthday, one black and one white.

There are numerous photos of family members together and separately outside on the deck. I remember going out on the deck as a young child. It was on the third floor of a four-story brownstone. The building had three apartments. My family occupied the duplex on the top two floors and two other families lived on the first and second floors. Later my parents had the deck covered with wood, but in those years, it was tarred like our roof. Every year on New Year's Eve, the other families in the building joined us to listen to the boom of the foghorns of the ships in New York Harbor as they all sounded at midnight. We used empty bottles as noisemakers, pressing our bottom lips against the cool glass spouts and blowing across the tops to make our own foghorn sounds.

***

When I still couldn't come up with any memories connected with my vision, Pierre suggested that on my next trip back to Brooklyn during spring break, I ask my parents what they remembered about my childhood.

I spoke with my father first. I explained that I was still having trouble in therapy remembering much about my childhood and wanted to hear what he could tell me. I sat down next to him in the living room on the long honey-colored couch, facing the brick fireplace, with a marble coffee table in between. In many families, living rooms are off limits to children; in our house it was only the couch that was to be treated with special care. No one was allowed to have food while sitting on it—of course my brother and I always did when my parents weren't around. Cindy, our salt and pepper miniature Schnauzer, wasn't allowed on the couch at all. She knew she wasn't because she always jumped down when she heard the family come home. But we could see the imprint on one of the cushions, marking where she slept while we were away.

My father sat in the corner of the couch with one leg crossed over the other and I sat next to him, my legs folded under me. With a little quiver in his voice and a pained expression, he said he'd done something when I was a baby that he'd felt guilty about ever since. As soon as he said that, I sat up straighter and leaned forward, anxious for anything that might shed light on my vision.

"I was home alone with you and you just wouldn't stop crying. I feel terrible about it, but out of desperation, I put a pillow over your face. I've felt guilty about it ever since." His forehead furrowed, he looked down, a little bent over, appearing smaller; his voice was softer than usual.

I sat there unfazed, with no change of expression. I asked him if there was anything else he remembered. I was so desperate to hear my father tell me something that would explain my vision that I was disappointed—as if he'd merely told me he'd once accidentally given me milk instead of orange juice.

Later that day, I spoke to my mother. She sat in the same place my father had on the couch, and stared straight ahead in silence for a moment. Then she casually said, "I remember that you hated to spend time alone as a child. And when you were about six years old, you were depressed." She didn't say anything about wondering why I was depressed or if she'd attempted to get me help. Unlike what my father shared, hearing this felt like important data. Looking back, it seems bizarre that I didn't follow up with any questions. The way she described me at that age felt as if she had seen me as deficient in some way. That caught me off guard and might explain why I didn't follow that thread. I came away disappointed that I hadn't gotten the information I was looking for.

Hypnosis

After working with Pierre for about six months, I was still unable to surface any memories that could lead to the source of my vision. I was determined to find out exactly what happened to me as a child. Finally, he suggested hypnosis.

There is a great deal of controversy surrounding hypnosis. There have been numerous instances in which therapists used suggestion to lead clients to create memories. The hypnosis I experienced was different. Pierre asked me open-ended questions without any suggestions other than those to help me relax. It wasn't like in the movies where people are unaware of their surroundings and can be made to cluck like a chicken. Nor was it the kind of hypnosis used to help individuals break a habit like smoking, using the power of suggestion to replace the desire to smoke with the feeling that smoking is repulsive. The goal was simply to get me into a relaxed state that would enable me to access memories I may have repressed. Once I was able to get into a trance quickly, he arranged for us to meet in a different office, one with a couch I could lie down on.

I took a bus to this new location in Boston. Walking rapidly along the street trying to find the right building number, my heart rate quickened. I don't know why but I had the impression that in this single session, I was going to bring back a ton of memories and solve the mystery of my vision. I thought this experience would be the key to everything.

The room was just large enough for a couch and a chair. I lay down on the couch and Pierre sat in the chair next to me. As he spoke in a slow, even, deep tone of voice, I relaxed and went into a trance. I felt completely calm and my mind felt comfortably blank.

"OK Deb, I want you to go back to your earliest childhood experience and tell me where you are and what's happening."

"I can see the brick house across the street from the Brooklyn Heights Promenade, where my family lived before I was born until I was about three years old. Our apartment was on the second or third floor. After you open the front door of the apartment, there's a hallway and the living room is at the end. There's a window that looks out over the front of the building and it's dark—it's late afternoon, but there are no lights on."

"How old are you?"

"I'm about one-and-a-half years old. I'm tiny and have short, straight, blond hair. I'm wearing a dress with short sleeves. The bodice is straight and close-fitting, but at the waist it widens out into a short skirt."

"Is anyone else there?"

"Just my father. It's quiet and I'm bored. I go to look for him because I feel lonely. I want to play with someone. I want some company.

"He's in the bedroom sitting on the side of the bed. There's a window behind him and the shades are down. There's a little light coming in, but his face and body are dark.

"I get into his lap. I want to be hugged and to cuddle. I hug him and it feels good. And then…and then, it doesn't feel good. He put one of his hands under my dress and he put his fingers inside me down there…I don't know what to do…I don't like it…I want him to stop."

I began to cry and my therapist said, "OK Deb, come on back to the present."

I came out of the trance feeling soiled and dirty, as if I was covered in a coating of filth that no washing could remove. I also felt deep shame. I was responsible for what happened. I was the one who had climbed into his lap. There must be something wrong with me to have that happen.

As I recorded this memory while writing this book, I started crying. I felt myself shrivel and become smaller and had to force myself to keep writing.

***

I wanted to know more. I was determined to discover as much as possible about what happened to me. In our next session, about a week later, I surfaced another memory.

"OK Deb, tell me about another childhood memory."

After a while, I said, "I'm in my bedroom but not in the same house. I'm in the brownstone we moved to when I was in second grade. I'm standing in my room on the side of my bed near the window. My father's standing on the other side of the bed with his back to the door."

"How old are you?"

"I'm about twelve years old. I'm skinny and wearing a striped T-shirt and jeans. My hair is long, straight and strawberry blond. I'm telling my father 'no.' I'm not going to let him touch me any more.

"He's angry…I'm scared…I want to get away from him, but he's standing in the way of the door.

"He comes to where I am. He grabs my ankles…He's dragging me around the room and shouting at me…I'm on my back and I can't get my feet away from him…I can't stop him."

"What is he saying?"

"I don't know."

"Do you know where your mother is?"

"She's downstairs, alone in the kitchen…drinking a Martini. She's hunched over, focusing on her drink."

Then I came out of the trance.

It seems strange for me to have an image of my mother in another room. But when Pierre asked me where she was, that image popped into my mind. Perhaps that was the way my mind made sense of her absence.

As I wrote this memory down, I felt the helplessness and terror of that incident. When I faced my father, my body was tense; I felt like a hunted animal trapped with no place to run.

Pierre and I felt we'd found confirmation that my vision was not a "screen," but represented reality. Painful as it was to experience these memories, once the hypnosis was over, it felt as if the pain were left behind. I experienced no anger or sadness, only resolution. I had no idea how many other feelings were simmering beneath my sense of relief.

***

Miguel graduated in May of 1981 and left Boston. We broke up that summer. That fall, I was scheduled to leave Boston for an internship and would be unable to continue working with Pierre. These two fragments were the sum total of the memories that I was able to surface. Before uncovering these memories, my vision was merely a symbol. These memories, however, felt concrete and tangible, making real the idea that my father had committed incest.

PARENTS LIKE MINE

I understand that incest takes place in families of all kinds. Nonetheless, it was difficult for me to reconcile how it could have happened in a family with parents like mine.

Mystery of Memory

Before they passed away, six weeks apart in 2012 and 2013, my parents spent a significant part of their lives working for social and racial justice. Their friends and acquaintances included Paul Robeson, John Oliver Killens, W.E.B. Dubois, Earl Robinson and Bella Abzug.

I was raised in an environment in which politics were discussed at length. From when I was as young as five or six, my parents took my brother and me to peace demonstrations. I remember standing somewhere on the Mall in Washington, DC, wearing a button saying, "Geneva, not genocide." I knew we were there for a peace march, but I didn't know what the button meant.

Once, my parents sent my brother and me out in the neighborhood to hand out campaign leaflets for Robert Kennedy. A woman came over to us, took my brother by the shoulders and shook him. "Your parents should be ashamed of themselves for supporting Kennedy. Stop handing these out and go home." Her voice was sharp and loud.

When my brother and I came home, I told our parents about what happened. "This mean lady shook Aaron. It was scary. She told us not to give the papers out anymore and that you should be ashamed of yourselves."

I saw the color come into their faces and one of them said, "She was probably a Republican. She's just an ignorant person who doesn't know what she's talking about."

In my family being Republican was tantamount to a sin. When Barry Goldwater ran against Lyndon Johnson in the 1960's, I recall my mother talking on the phone to a friend of hers: "If Goldwater wins, we may need to think about leaving the U.S. and moving to Canada."

Being a Democrat and standing up for one's beliefs were traditions in our household. As early as the fifth or sixth grade, with our parents' support, my friend Laura and I refused to say the Pledge of Allegiance partly because of the words "one nation under God" (my parents were staunch atheists) and partly because we didn't believe the U.S. lived up to its claim of standing for "liberty and justice for all."

Throughout most of my childhood, my family didn't buy California grapes to support the United Farm Workers boycott, or products manufactured by Dow Chemical because they made Napalm for use in Vietnam. In high school, I followed my parents' lead and engaged in a variety of social justice activities, handing out leaflets and attending marches against the Vietnam War, volunteering at the Fortune Society, a prison reform organization, and working on political campaigns for progressive candidates like Bella Abzug and Al Lowenstein.

I recall when my father told me about the Scottsboro Boys, the nine black teenagers who were framed and convicted of rape in Alabama in 1941 by an all-white jury. My father was sitting at his desk in the study, opening mail.

"What's that?"

"It's a letter about the Scottsboro Boys."

"Who are they?"

"They were a group of black teenagers who were accused of a crime they hadn't committed and sent to jail just because they were black."

I don't remember anything else he told me, but that conversation brought home to me the reality of injustice in the court system based on race.

I remember watching a gruesome documentary about the Holocaust that included a scene with piles of skeletons.

"What's that?"

"Those are the remains of Jews who were killed by German Nazis during the War."

Not believing that anything like that was possible in recent history, I asked, "That was a long time ago, right?"

"It was a little over twenty years ago," one of them replied.

"You were alive when that happened?" I asked in shock.

"Yes. Jews have been persecuted throughout history. In Russia and Poland, there were pogroms, where Jews were massacred, and they were killed during the Crusades as well."

Mystery of Memory

***

My mother had been politically active from a young age—both her parents were progressive, supporting unions, civil rights, and peace. In 1940, because of her involvement with the American Students Union as an undergraduate at Brooklyn College, she was subpoenaed to appear before the Joint Legislative Committee to Investigate the Educational System of the State of New York. This committee, informally known as the Rapp-Coudert Committee, investigated "subversive activities" in the city schools, trying to expose instructors and administrators who were communists. The attorney representing the Committee tried without success to get my mother to admit to being a member of the Young Communist League.

Decades later, my mother was interviewed by a Brooklyn College professor interested in the history of the American Students Union. My mother described her experience:

[The] Rapp-Coudert [Committee] did two things: it frightened me and afterwards I think it was a kind of strengthening experience. After that I was not afraid to go see anyone in any position for anything. [The experience] made political action an important part of my life.

In the 1970s, when my mother worked at the New York City Department of the Aging, she stood up against then-Brooklyn Borough President Howard Golden. She was responsible for contracting out nutrition programs for senior centers and had made plans to remove a program from a facility with broken steps and a non-functioning toilet. Golden called to protest her taking the center from a rabbi who was "important to me." She didn't back down and said that she "rather enjoyed that kind of encounter." These stories are family heirlooms to me; artifacts of the social justice legacy my parents left me, for which I am deeply grateful.

My heart hurt when I read the transcript of this interview years later, after she had passed away. I realized that the strong woman my mother was outside our home wasn't the same woman inside our home. In so many ways, she made herself small in comparison to my father.

"Mom, can you help me with this paper?"

"Ask your father. You know he's better at writing than me."

She was a true intellectual, and in my mind more intelligent than my father, but she always deferred to him. While I remember my mother talking about the incident with the Borough President, I don't remember seeing her stand up to my father about anything. She had a less direct way of getting what she wanted that I learnt about decades later when my parents were in their eighties. My father wanted to move out of their brownstone apartment because he thought it was too big. My mother loved it there, particularly because of the outdoor deck; she loved to garden.

"Mom, Dad says he wants to move to a smaller place. Do you want to move or stay here?"

"I want to stay here."

"Did you tell Daddy that?"

"No, I just go along and visit places he's considering and find things wrong with them." In the end, they never moved.

My mother's courage did not come from out of the blue. My grandmother was the first person in her family to go to college and she was one of six or seven women in a class with 200 men at Columbia University's College of Pharmacy. She later became chief of a hospital pharmacy. According to my mother, my grandmother marched in suffrage parades.

My father didn't come from a politically aware family and only became politically active when he started college at the City University of New York and was introduced to the Communist Party by a girlfriend.

***

When I was in elementary school, my parents and many of their friends worked to integrate the public school my brother and I attended. They supported a new experimental process known as "pairing," that involved combining two neighboring segregated elementary schools into a common school zone.

As a result of this pairing process, my elementary school in Brooklyn Heights was merged with one in the neighborhood known then as Farragut. Students from both neighborhoods attended one school from the first to fourth grade and the other for the fifth and sixth grades. Farragut was mainly an industrial area with few residential buildings other than a high-rise housing project.

We walked across Cadman Plaza Park to get to school, but it may as well have been walking to a different world. On one side of the park were brownstone-studded, tree-lined streets. On the other, the neighborhood was bleak and the sidewalks littered with garbage. The picture was clear; white people lived in nice neighborhoods and black people did not. I realized that I lived a life of privilege that I had done nothing to deserve. I thought it wasn't fair and felt in some way responsible, ashamed and guilty. The guilt and shame felt all my own; not that of all white people. I felt like I was the tainted one.

During that period, I went over to a friend's house after school. She lived in a small brick house in my neighborhood. We climbed two sets of stairs to reach her room on the third floor and sat down in a bay window that overlooked the street. We were talking about slavery because we'd been taught about it in class that day. She said, "Slavery wasn't as bad as the Holocaust. Slaves were able to stay alive, but Jews were killed."

She waited for me to agree, either because we were both Jewish or because we were both white. I said nothing, but felt staying silent was being disloyal to the black students in our class. Her statement felt wrong, but I didn't know what to say.

Many of my beliefs about racial justice were planted during that time. In addition to being in favor of the school pairing process, my parents also supported an initiative designed to provide communities with decision-making power in their local schools. When the school board in the predominantly black Ocean Hill-Brownsville neighborhood fired some teachers, almost all of whom were white and Jewish, the City's teachers' union went on strike demanding their reinstatement. My staunch labor- and union-supporting parents opposed the strike. In this case, the right of a black community to control its own school, and determine which teachers best served their children's educational achievement, trumped labor rights.

From a young age, my parents instilled in me the importance of leaving the world a better place and taking action in support of what's just and fair.

WHAT ELSE I KNOW ABOUT MY PARENTS

My mother would remove a splinter or put on a Band-Aid, but she didn't offer hugs or comforting words. When I was about nine years old, I experienced severe anxiety and apprehension every Sunday night. I went to my mother once to talk about it. She was seated at one end of the dining room table, papers spread all over, as usual—my parents dropped the mail and the newspaper there when they came home. I sat down. She looked up from what she was reading.

"Mommy, I don't feel good."

"What's the matter?"

"I don't know."

"What's wrong?"

"I just feel bad in my stomach."

"Do you think you're sick?"

"No, I just feel bad."

I wanted her to wrap me in her arms and rock me while telling me that everything was OK. Instead, she tried to determine the source of the anxiety.

"Well, are you worried about something?"

"No."

"Is someone bothering you at school?"

"No."

"Did your teacher do anything?"

"No."

I didn't know how to explain what I was feeling. Even now, it's difficult. It was an uncomfortable sensation in my solar plexus; a horrible mixture of guilt- and shame-tinged apprehension and anxiety, as if I'd done something wrong. I don't remember how this incident ended but I continued to experience this on Sunday nights until I went away to college.

I don't remember my mother using any terms of endearment with me. I do remember a time in junior high school when she got angry with me. I was on my way up the stairs to my bedroom. My mother pointed out a pair of shoes on the bottom step.

"Deborah, bring those shoes upstairs with you."

"I can't now, my hands are full."

"You're a real pill, you know that?"

The incident doesn't stand out as particularly insensitive. It probably represents a fairly normal conversation between a mother and a pre-teen. But the word "pill" stands out in contrast to the scarcity of words of affection.

Similarly, when I try to recall words of wisdom my mother shared with me, the only thing I can come up with is how, as a young girl walking with my mother, she would constantly tell me to hold my stomach in and walk straight or I'd have bad posture.

I don't remember many hugs or kisses either. I do recall one evening when I had trouble falling asleep. My mother pulled up a chair and took my hand in hers; she moved her thumb back and forth rhythmically while she hummed and stared into space.

People who knew my mother described her as stoic. A friend of mine, who knew my mother all her life, shared with me that she always experienced her as "repressed." They also described her as elegant. I have a picture of my mother and father dancing at a party they attended. The photo was clearly posed. One side of their bodies faces the camera. My father's left hand is stretched out with my mother's right hand resting gently in his palm. My mother's left hand is on his right shoulder, her long, slender fingers facing the camera. Her hair is cut short enough that her earlobes are visible, her long silver earrings reflecting the light coming from somewhere above them. My father is facing the camera and smiling, but my mother isn't; her chin is lifted, her eyes looking to the side. Around her neck is a necklace of sedate gold beads.

Whenever my parents had parties, my brother and I were bustled upstairs to bed. From my room, I heard glasses tinkling, and murmuring voices from below. I'd always wish I was allowed to go down and watch, but I wasn't. Once, when I sat on the stairway to peek, I saw my mother smoking a cigarette. I'd never seen her smoke before. I mentioned it the next day and she said she used to smoke but quit when she found out it was dangerous.

When my mother was in the eighth grade, her class created a book with future predictions about each student. My mother's classmates wrote:

The odor of oil paints coming from an open door directs us to our classmate's studio. We reach the threshold and our first glance discloses the tidiness of the room. The walls are hung with pictures; the shelves are filled with beautiful clay models. The table nearby is strewn with papers. We look sideways and we see some poems on the table, undoubtedly written by our friend in spare moments. Our glance wanders further on, and near the large window stands our classmate, tall and slender, busily painting away at her easel. Perhaps you already know whom we've come to visit? Down go the brushes and the paints and before a minute is over we are busily talking about old times and we forget that our hostess is the famous artist the world knows her to be. To us she is simply the quiet and charming girl we knew.

I wondered who my mother had been before she married my father. In how many ways did she make herself less than who she really was? My mother was a fabulous artist, but she refused to believe that she was, and only allowed herself to create beautiful hand-painted birthday cards over the years. I have one of them framed in my home because it is so lovely.

***

While neither of my parents were the type to be delighted by babies, my father's eyes lit up and his face softened around kittens or puppies. Yet he could also explode in rage, with anger pouring out of him like steam from a kettle. I recall an incident my brother told me about when we were both in high school and my parents found a joint in his room. My father was enraged, dragged him by his hair and threw him up against a wall. My brother laughed about it when he told me what happened. It frightened me.

My father wasn't particularly good with his hands, despite the workbench in the back attic. I think it was my maternal grandfather, the mechanical engineer, who gave it to my father as a gift. I don't know all of what my father used it for, but I do remember a phase of cutting wine bottles to make drinking glasses. He had a large assortment of tools—screwdrivers, hammers, saws, nuts, bolts, screws, hooks, pliers, wrenches—and yet I have no memory of him using any of them to do more than hang a picture. My father was more interested in things intellectual than mechanical.

While people described my mother as stoic, they described my father as driven. He was a bit of a control freak. He was fretful if things weren't done exactly the way he did them.

Whenever I tried to load the dishwasher after dinner at my parents' house, he'd say, "Just leave it on the counter."

"It's OK. I don't want to leave work for you and Mom to do later."

"No, I'll do it. I have a special way of putting the dishes in."

During the last year or so of his life, when my father was no longer able to drive, I took my parents to all their medical appointments. Each time we neared a doctor's office, he sat up straight in the passenger seat, swiveled his head around, eyes darting anxiously to find a parking place even though I'd repeatedly told him I was going to drop them off and then find somewhere to park. As my parents exited the car, he'd give me specific directions about which streets were likely to have spaces available.

His dream had always been to be a writer, to write short stories or a novel. He told me about pieces he'd written and sent to a neighbor who worked as an editor in a major publishing house. He hoped she might help him, but her feedback was not encouraging. My father was raised working class; working as an executive at a major Madison Avenue advertising firm brought him into a foreign world. At first, he didn't know what an expense account was, let alone that he had one at his disposal.

I'm not sure how he rationalized his earlier communist ideology with working in advertising, the epitome of capitalism. Perhaps it was the only way for him to do the work he loved and still support his family. The extent of his published writing was a number of articles, a short book about direct mail marketing, and a few letters to editors.

I know little about my father's father, but from what I do know, he wasn't successful in supporting his family. My paternal grandmother came from a middle-class family and of all her sisters she was the only one who married a man from the working class. I imagine my father was determined to be different. He didn't have the luxury of doing work that was in complete alignment with his political views.

My father was also deeply impacted by living through the Depression. He had a scarcity mentality and found it almost impossible to throw anything away. "You never know when you might need it," he'd say if I tried to get him to let go of anything. Shortly before he passed away, I was finally able to convince him to let me throw out the onionskin and carbon paper he had kept for decades.

***

There were times when I experienced my father as lecherous and inappropriate. I remember one night when we watched TV together, whenever a woman on the screen was wearing a low-cut or revealing outfit, his eyes glazed over, almost as if he were in a momentary trance.

"Daddy, all you do is stare at the women on the screen."

His reply felt humiliating. "Well, they have breasts, you don't."

Once when I was around 15 or 16 years old, my mother and I had gone shopping. We came home with a number of shopping bags and took them into my parents' bedroom. "Why don't you try on your new clothes and show them to Daddy?" my mother asked.

I put on a skirt and blouse. I felt grown-up in my new clothes and went into the dining room where my father sat reading. He glanced up to look at me, taking me in from head to toe. I didn't feel my father's pride. I felt like he was looking at me the way he looked at women on TV sometimes. I went back to my parents' bedroom to change and didn't model any of the other clothes we'd bought.

Around the same time, I was riding in the car alone with my father. "You know I tried to date your mother when she was living in Washington, DC, during the War, but she wouldn't have it. I ended up getting married to another woman but it only lasted a few months. After the divorce, my ex-wife and her mother came to the apartment and cleared it out." He didn't tell me why they got divorced and I didn't ask.

At some point in the conversation, he told me with some pride that he had never cheated on my mother and said, "You know, I've always been attracted to physically strong women."

I wondered why he told me he'd never had an affair. And why did he want me to know he was attracted to strong women? I took pride in being athletic and strong: I played volleyball, hockey, and basketball. I did gymnastics and practiced judo. Was that his way of saying I was in some way like the women he was attracted to? Not knowing what to say, I just said, "Oh."

Some Childhood Memories

I was the "goody-two-shoes" of the family. I always followed the rules and overall was well behaved. My brother Aaron was considered the "problem child." Once, when he was in fifth or sixth grade, he threatened to jump off the roof and kill himself. My parents took him to a psychiatrist. On at least one occasion the whole family attended a session with this doctor. I remember sitting in the waiting room, then being in a room with the psychiatrist, all of us being asked a lot of questions. I don't remember any of the questions or answers. None of it made sense to me. I just knew we were there to "help" my brother.

Starting around that time, I saw myself as his protector, even though he was two years older than me. He wasn't popular in school and wore glasses with thick black frames. One day I was standing in front of our house with some other kids from school. An older brother of a boy my age said something referring to my brother. I don't remember his words, but I told him, "Please don't say mean things about my brother."

In our teen years, I always did my homework, never did drugs, and wasn't rebellious. Aaron was the rebel. In high school, with his long hair—past his shoulders—he often refused to study or do homework and tried almost every drug available in the 1970's. In high school, I pleaded with Aaron to do his homework so he wouldn't get in trouble. When we were supposed to go someplace with my parents and he refused to go, I begged him to come so "Daddy won't get angry and punish you." Aaron always got a spanking when he was punished. I may have gotten punished a few times but I was never spanked.

**

Sometimes I took the blame for things my brother did. Once, we were in my room and he was swinging a yo-yo. The yo-yo knocked into and broke the glass globe of the overhead light on my bedroom ceiling. "Oh no! Deb, please tell Mom and Dad that you broke it. You know I'll get punished, but they won't get mad at you."

Our parents came home a few hours later and I told them, "I have to tell you something. I was playing with a yo-yo in my room and I accidentally broke the glass on the ceiling light. I'm really sorry."

"That's OK," my father said gruffly. "Just be careful next time."

Some days when my parents left us alone, Aaron bullied me. I don't remember exactly what he did. I just remember running to one of the bathrooms (the only rooms that had locks on the door) to lock myself in to get away from him. Then, just before my parents were due to come home, he'd beg me, "Please don't tell on me. I promise to be nice. Please don't tell." On the other hand, "telling on him" did me no good anyway. One day I was in my room and asked him to leave.

"I don't want you in here. Please get out."

"No, I don't want to."

"It's my room and I asked you to leave so get out!"

"No, I'm not leaving. Make me." I felt powerless. When he kept refusing to leave, I yelled downstairs to my parents, "Mom, Dad, Aaron won't leave my room! Make him leave!" After no response, I screamed, "Mooooom, Daaaad, tell him to get out of my room!" When they still didn't respond, I finally screamed at the top of my lungs, "Get out of my room!" I yelled until I was hoarse. He didn't leave until he got bored of making me miserable. As soon as he left, I moved my bureau in front of my bedroom door so he couldn't come in. When he realized that I'd closed the door to keep him out, he tried to open it. "I don't want you to come in here. Stay out!" I told him, but he put all his weight against the door and pushed his way in just to spite me.

***

Some incidents of a sexual nature took place with my brother and a neighbor, but I would include them in the category of children "playing doctor." I was about nine years old and our neighbor, Samuel, was about four years older than me. My brother and I were skinny. Samuel was kind of husky, with dark curly hair. Samuel suggested we play in my brother's room. The three of us ended up naked. I remember lying across Samuel's lap, him caressing my butt while my brother just sat there.

Shortly after that, the three of us were playing in the yard with the other kids from the building. Samuel pulled my brother and me aside. He told me to make up some excuse to the other kids about why we were going back into the house. The first time it happened, it seemed innocent to me. This time, however, it didn't. Something about it felt wrong, but I felt like I couldn't say "no" because I hadn't said "no" before.

We went to my brother's room and got undressed. Almost as soon as we took our clothes off, my mother knocked on the door. We all jumped under the sheets of my brother's bed. She opened the door and said, "Deborah, come out right now!" Then she left the room, shutting the door behind her.

I jumped into my slip, more like a white cotton sundress, and came out into the hallway. My mother was standing outside the door. She took me down the hall to the laundry room where she furtively whispered, "Were you naked in there?"

"No," I lied, "I had my slip on."

With a taut face, she said, "What you were doing in there is wrong."

She didn't say anything to my brother or Samuel, who were both older than me. Whatever had happened was my responsibility. With downcast eyes and a red face, I slunk into my room.

When I think about these incidents with my brother and the neighbor, although I felt ashamed, there was no sense of being violated or betrayed. The sense of being responsible, however, felt familiar.

My mother responded in a similar fashion when I had an experience with an adult pervert in the neighborhood. I was sitting on the front stoop. A man holding two briefcases, one in each hand, approached me and said he needed help getting his keys out of his pocket because his hands were full. I put my hand in his right front pocket and found no keys. He kept telling me to move my hand to the left. Finally, I realized he was trying to get me to touch his penis. I took my hand out of his pocket and said, "Sorry, I can't find your keys." Then I walked away from him and ran back up the stoop to go home. Upstairs in our apartment, I told my mother what had happened.

She pulled me roughly into the bathroom, turned on the tap and washed my hands. "Don't ever let that happen again!"

II. The Confrontation

I MOVE TO ALASKA

At Northeastern Law School, we had what was called a "Co-op Program" that involved alternating academic study with full-time employment (or internships) each quarter. As long as you were able to find law-related employment, you could go wherever you wanted. In March of 1982, when I was a third-year law student, I went to Anchorage, Alaska on a whim, to work for a law firm. One of Miguel's closest friends, Rob, had moved there after he graduated the year before. We'd become good friends during the spring of his third year when we both worked in Boston, meeting for lunch regularly. He convinced me to take an internship in Anchorage. Why not? I figured I'd be able to hang out with Rob and it would be interesting to go someplace where polar bears patrolled the streets downtown.

Before going to Alaska, I'd been a city girl through and through. When my friends in Boston suggested weekends at "the Cape," I didn't understand why they would want to leave the city. Boston was where the fun was. We could go to Faneuil Hall to shop and eat, we could go to the movies, anything you needed was in walking distance or accessible by public transportation. I'd grown up in New York City, surrounded by skyscrapers; everything around me was man-made. Anchorage was nothing like that.

Huge snow-capped mountains surrounded the city in all directions. A two-minute walk from the center of town took me to the edge of a bay with nothing manmade in sight. I stayed blocks from the downtown area in a log cabin surrounded by trees on three sides and a view of the water on the fourth side. The natural beauty all around left me in awe.

Rob took me on a short trip out of town to see Portage Glacier. We drove down the sole highway south of Anchorage. It was a two-lane road and with one wrong turn we'd either crash into the wall of rock on one side, or fall into the gorge below on the other side. As we crossed a bridge on the highway, Rob explained that the color of the robin's-egg-blue stream below was the result of silt from the melting glaciers. When we came out of the mountains, the land was flat, with fields and trees on either side. It was fall. The color of the trees ranged from deep yellow to rusty red, not yet naked, as they would be in winter. We pulled over so Rob could fish; it was late in the season, but we could still see some salmon swimming fiercely upstream as they attempted to return to their birthplace. As I stood there watching Rob fishing down river, the sheer grandeur of the mountains left me with a sense that there must be a power in the world larger than me. I was moved by the purity and simplicity of the beauty surrounding me.

To the surprise of my family and friends, I decided to move to Anchorage permanently. After completing my academic requirements the following winter, I spent my final internship during the spring of 1982 at another law firm in Anchorage. After graduation, I left behind everything and everyone I knew to move to Alaska.

Halfway through my flight to Anchorage, I wondered what the hell I was thinking. Why in the world did I decide to move not only to the other side of the nation, but outside of the Continental United States? Then, as the plane descended into the airport, I saw Anchorage's majestic mountains, the pristine snow, and glaciers covering the mountains. It was pure, untouched nature; my body relaxed, my breathing slowed down, and I felt a sense of deep grounding. A hitherto unknown sense of calm, safety and certainty enveloped me. All my fears and doubts were gone; I was coming home.

It was summer when I arrived. The days were almost endless until midnight, when the sky turned to dusk. I lived in a one-bedroom apartment on the ground floor of a tree-hidden wooden house steps away from Cook Inlet. Looking out the picture window, I saw white whales in the distance while I studied for the bar examination.

***

Feelings Begin to Surface

With a month left to study for the bar, my mother called, "Deb, how about I visit you in Alaska for my vacation next month after your exam is over?"

"OK. I'll have time to show you around." I welcomed the idea of spending time alone with my mother.

A week later, she called again. "Daddy wants to come next month too, so we'll both be coming." At first, I didn't think much about what it would be like to have my father visit as well. Soon after I got off the phone, however, my chest tightened and I started to feel anxious. In that moment, it became clear to me why Anchorage felt more like home than Brooklyn. Anchorage was untouched. My father had never been there and nothing about it even remotely reminded me of him. Having him come to Anchorage would be a desecration of my pure haven.

I had no intention of confronting my parents about either my vision or the memories. I worried that if I did, they would feel ashamed and humiliated. For some reason, I even feared that they would want to commit suicide as a result. At the least, I imagined my mother might want to divorce my father. I had no desire to hurt either of them or ruin their lives. But, I didn't want my father to come and needed to figure out a way to tell my mother.

After deciding what to say, I called my mother back. "Mom, I've been dealing with some issues about Daddy in therapy and don't feel comfortable having him come visit with you. I'd really like you to come by yourself."

Her response was matter of fact. "I can't tell Daddy not to come. He already made his vacation plans."

I was devastated. I did not want my father to step foot in Alaska. I called a friend of mine, a fellow Northeastern alum with whom I'd shared my memories. He'd graduated a few years before me and we'd gotten to know each other when I interned in Anchorage. When I started crying he told me to come to his house. I went and cried in his arms, alternating between feeling anger at my mother and distraught about how violated I'd feel by my father's presence.

Nonetheless, as the dutiful daughter, I planned a trip for them. While they were in Anchorage, I introduced them to my boyfriend, Alejandro, a real estate agent. He did his best to impress my parents. Treating them with the utmost respect, he took the three of us out to dinner at Simon & Seaforts Restaurant, the best place in town for seafood. During dinner, my parents said little. Even my father, who is usually voluble even with strangers, didn't say much. I knew that in their view, Alejandro wasn't an "intellectual," and they admired intellectualism above all else. He didn't readily engage in the same topics of conversation that they did: politics mainly.

When my parents and I took an overnight trip to the nearby town of Homer, I invited along two Northeastern students who were interning in Anchorage. We'd become friends and I didn't want to travel alone with my parents. During the drive down and dinner with my parents, I sensed the anger at my father building.

In our room after dinner, I shared my feelings with my friends.

"I can't stand having him here and I can't say anything about it."

"Can't you say something, even just to your mother?" one of them asked.

"I don't even know what I could say. I just feel so tense and irritable around him." Confronting my parents with my memories was still out of the question, fearful as I was that it would lead them to suicide.

Mystery of Memory

Our next trip, to Denali National Park, didn't go well. There were four of us because the daughter of family friends, Jennifer, who also happened to be in Anchorage, joined us. We all went in my parents' rental car and I drove. My mother and Jennifer sat in the back. My father sat in the front; he shifted position constantly and kept staring at my hands on the steering wheel. "Deborah, let me drive," he said. He couldn't stand not being in total control and I didn't want to give him control.

"Why? My driving is completely safe," I replied.

"I don't like the way you don't keep both hands on the steering wheel."

"OK, fine, you can drive." I abruptly pulled the car onto the shoulder and exited the car in a huff. Both of us were edgy and cross. My father knew I hadn't wanted him to come, but we never broached the topic. I couldn't wait for my father to leave; my anger was growing rapidly. This was the beginning of my realization that my feelings about what happened were not all resolved.

***

Shortly after my parents' visit, I began a yearlong clerkship with a judge on the Alaska Criminal Court of Appeals. I was still in touch with Pierre. We didn't have therapy sessions over the phone (long distance calls were fairly expensive at the time), but we stayed in touch. I told him I felt violated and angry when my father came to Anchorage. I was also frustrated that no other memories had surfaced. Pierre assured me that over time more would come. He suggested I find and join a support group for women incest survivors. I found a group sponsored by Parents United, an organization that provides support for all family members impacted by incest; children who have been sexually abused, adults who were abused as children, other family members, and perpetrators.

The adult survivors group was all women. They met weekly and talked about how being molested affected their lives. Meetings took place in a dreary, basement room in a church. In the hallway, was a table with a coffee urn, paper cups, sugar and Coffee-mate.

When I first attended a meeting, the women were sitting in a circle on metal folding chairs. I took fleeting looks around the room, trying to get a feeling for how the group operated. While I was hesitant at first, the group was welcoming. After some brief introductions, the floor was open to anyone who wanted to share. Individuals could remain silent and simply listen if they preferred. At first I just listened as others talked about their experiences. The feelings of anger, sadness, betrayal and deep shame that they shared resonated inside me. I felt an immediate sense of kinship with the women in the room even though with some, being survivors may have been the only thing we had in common.

I found it empowering to talk with these women, but I was disheartened as well. The other members of the group seemed to have clear memories, whereas all I had was my vision and two memory fragments. I couldn't say exactly what happened to me or for how long. Since undergoing the hypnosis, no other memories had emerged. But all sorts of painful feelings and emotions were starting to surface. As it was still early in the process, I assumed that with more time, other memories would emerge.

Shame and Other Sensations

At Pierre's suggestion, I found a new therapist, Kathryn. She was a member of a women's therapy collective. When I expressed frustration about not being able to surface any more memories of being molested, Kathryn pointed out that this was because when my father fondled me, I was pre-verbal. My mind couldn't express or even conceptualize what was happening to me. She also told me that it was common for incest survivors to repress memories.

In our sessions, I shared with her the painful feelings that were surfacing: anger, intense shame, a sense of betrayal and violation, as well as sadness. Early on, the focus was on my father.

"I feel so robbed. When I see little girls walking down the street holding their fathers' hands, my chest contracts and I feel like crying.

I envy them; I can see the way they walk, feeling safe and secure, knowing their fathers will protect them from harm. I feel grief and a sense of loss. Why couldn't I have had that kind of father? Not only wasn't he a safe haven, but he was the one I needed protection from. When I think about that, then I get angry and feel such fury.

"Looking back, I realize that once I started dating as a teenager, I never had more than a few weeks between boyfriends. Anytime I didn't have a boyfriend, I felt depressed and worthless, regardless of who initiated the end of the relationship. Having a man in my life was the only thing that made me feel safe, protected and loved."

Later, the focus switched to my mother.

"I just wish she'd been more available to me. I didn't feel any warmth from her; she was cool and unemotional. I think that's why I was looking to my father to cuddle with me when I was little. All I wanted was to climb into his lap and have him hold me. But I didn't expect or want what came with that. I don't think his touching me was based on sexual attraction. I think he was also looking for warmth, but was unable to separate the two."

There was a significant period of time during which I experienced deep grief about my mother not being there for me, and even some empathy for my father, seeing him as similar to me, looking for warmth that he wasn't receiving from my mother.

Other times, I dealt with feeling unclean, damaged and ashamed. There's a quote in Toni Morrison's *Beloved* that sums it up. "Dirty you so bad you couldn't like yourself anymore. Dirty you so bad you forgot who you were and couldn't think it up."

Kathryn explained to me that when children are molested, they blame themselves, believing that they asked for/were somehow responsible for what happened. This self-blame then leads to a sense of being inherently bad. That was certainly how I often felt.

In addition to individual therapy, Kathryn's collective also offered a number of workshops and group therapy options. Because I was struggling with intense feelings of shame, I decided to attend a full-day Shame Workshop for women, offered by another therapist in the collective.

We sat on the floor in a circle. Each of us introduced ourselves and shared why we had come. Then we did some role-playing; participants acted out traumatic and shame-inducing experiences. I chose the incident of my father dragging me around my room when I was twelve. After describing the attack and simply saying that my mother wasn't in the room, I selected two other participants to play the roles of my mother and father.

For the role-play, I lay on the floor on my back, the woman playing the role of my father held my ankles. The woman playing the role of my mother stood off to the side. After my "father" dragged me around, the two other participants were asked how they'd felt. The woman who'd played my mother said, "I just felt like going into the kitchen to get a Martini."

Eerily, that image matched the one I saw when describing that incident to Pierre.

***

The therapy collective also had a group for female incest survivors. I joined it and as with the first survivors' group I attended, felt a connection with the other women in the group.

In one session, I experienced tightness in my throat. The therapist leading the group asked me to lie down on the floor, close my eyes and focus on the body sensation I was experiencing. As I concentrated, I sensed my larynx being squeezed as if a belt was tied around it. A feeling of grief came over me and I started crying. After a few minutes, the tightness loosened and I sat up.

I had another strange and frightening experience around that time. Alejandro and I broke up, and few months after, I began a relationship with a Panamanian man who was about seven feet tall. Tall as he was, he was gentle and soft-spoken. We never had sex, but we slept in the same bed together once. I woke up in the middle of the night. As I took in this massive form next to me, I felt tiny and helpless. My body tensed, my pulse quickened, and my breath was shallow; I was terrified and felt like I was in danger. This feeling of terror and powerlessness felt familiar. It lasted for about five minutes. I reminded myself that I had no reason to fear him. However, when I woke up, I knew that despite his gentleness, I couldn't be physically intimate with him without being triggered.

On another occasion, I was home alone and feeling anxious without knowing why. I lay down on the carpet in my living room, closed my eyes and paid attention to my breath as Pierre had taught me; I entered a trance. At first I wasn't aware of my body. Then I felt my body become small, as if I were an infant. I sensed a weight over my face and chest. I struggled to breathe. My heart rate quickened and I came out of the trance as if waking from a nightmare. I felt as if I had re-experienced the incident my father described when he held a pillow over my face to stop me from crying when I was an infant.

It's difficult to explain what these incidents felt like to me. I had no explanation for where they could be coming from; there was nothing going on in the present moment to which they could be attributed.

THE CONFRONTATION

Despite my growing anger, betrayal and grief, I managed to compartmentalize these feelings and maintain a relationship with my parents. I still hadn't told either of them about the memories I surfaced during my hypnosis sessions in Boston. I felt I could handle what was happening to me on my own; I felt in some way stronger emotionally than my parents. However, in November of 1982, months after my parents had visited me, they asked to talk with Pierre. "We're worried about you. You're all alone in Anchorage and we want to be sure you're OK."

"Why? I'm fine, but if it will make you feel better, sure, you can talk to him."

It didn't occur to me at the time how inappropriate it was for parents to request to speak with their adult child's therapist. I called Pierre, who agreed to speak to my parents and reassure them that I was OK. My assumption was that he would have a five- to ten-minute conversation with them, simply to allay any fears they had. A few weeks later, Pierre called.

"Deb, I talked with your parents."

"What happened?" I asked, expecting him to tell me that my parents were sufficiently reassured.

"I was going to be in New York and I arranged to visit them when I came to town." That was a surprise to me.

"I went to their house and shortly after I arrived, suggested that your father and I take a walk. I told him that you had memories of being molested by him when you were a child."

On the one hand I was shocked that Pierre had told my parents about my memories without my permission. On the other hand, I felt relief that I no longer had to carry the secret. I trusted Pierre and while I was taken aback, I wasn't angry.

"How did my father respond?"

"He told me, he didn't have any memory of that, but that he knew that people can repress memories. Then he said, 'Let's go back and ask Deborah's mother.'"

"That's what he said? He wasn't shocked or surprised?"

"No, it was strange how calm he was. We went back to the house, and I told your mother the same thing. She didn't look surprised either. She just said she had no knowledge of that taking place and she'd have to think about it."

"They were completely calm? Didn't they get upset at all?" I asked, feeling confused and shocked.

"No, it was weird. Both of them were composed and unperturbed."

I couldn't fathom that. How could they have been so calm and cool? "So, did you say anything else?"

"No, I just asked them not to contact you about our conversation, but to let you be the one to reach out to contact them."

I was floored that neither of them had expressed pain of any kind—certainly not the suicidal reaction I had anticipated. Now I was mad.

I'd been worrying about their feelings for years, and based on what Pierre shared with me, they appeared to have little or no concern for mine.

***

I contacted my parents a few weeks after talking with Pierre. We may have had more than one conversation, but I remember demanding my father acknowledge that there had been some kind of sexual contact when I was a child. I was adamant because I felt I'd been carrying a family secret on my own and needed to share the burden. Now that it was clear my parents weren't going to fall apart, I wasn't willing to shoulder the pain on my own.

Despite what he said when he spoke with Pierre, my father wrote shortly after, and unequivocally denied that he had done anything.

We are very willing to do whatever you would like us to do to help, and I wish it were that easy. Pierre had suggested that the four of us get together and we were looking forward to it as at least a step in trying to straighten out things. But, Deb, when you tell us that, before we can do this, we or I must first tell you that something you think took place actually took place, this would mean I would have to say something which is absolutely not true.

Obviously repeating what I have already said is not going to change something that has been disturbing you all this time. I know that I would have been carrying a deep guilt if anything resembling what you think happened had ever occurred. I hope you will believe me that I never had any feelings or acted toward you in any but a paternal fashion. To say it even more directly, in case you think I am trying to talk around it with words: I never in any way had or tried to have sexual contact with you.

Reading this letter today, my father's response sounds caring and reasonable under the circumstances. I was incapable of seeing it that way. Nothing short of an admission would satisfy me. Having found that therapy had helped me access some memories and feelings that had been buried for years, I asked my father to meet with a therapist to see if he might discover some memories of his own. He agreed to do so.

***

My parents and I had sporadic conversations after that. In October of 1983, my mother called to tell me her father passed away. I was sad and disappointed that I hadn't had a chance to say goodbye to him; the last time I had called my grandparents, he hadn't felt well enough to come to the phone. I made plans to go back to New York for the funeral. My mother wanted me to stay at home but I decided to stay with a friend despite my mother's promise that "there is nothing to worry about."

Although I didn't tell him why, Aaron knew I didn't want to stay with our parents. He invited me to spend the night before the funeral at the apartment in Manhattan he shared with his girlfriend Sarah, so we could go to the funeral together. Like me, Sarah has a pale complexion and straight strawberry blonde hair although hers is redder than mine. On the morning of the funeral, my brother, his girlfriend and I took a taxi to the Riverside Memorial Chapel, the Jewish funeral home my family used. The taxi pulled up to the sidewalk in front of the entrance on Amsterdam Avenue. I saw my father standing on the sidewalk. Sarah got out of the car first and my father immediately hugged her.

I exited the car right after Sarah did, feeling nervous about seeing my father. He glanced my way, but didn't recognize me. It was almost like being slapped. It left me feeling worthless. Only after I tapped him on the shoulder did he acknowledge me. Then we hugged and all of us walked together into the funeral home.

The rest of the family and close friends were in a small room off the chapel prior to the service. When I entered, I saw my mother talking to Lily, her oldest childhood friend. Lily lived in Maine and hadn't seen me since I was a child. I walked over and stood next to my mother but didn't interrupt their conversation. When I came up to her, my mother looked over at me for a quick moment. Despite looking directly at me, she had a blank look on her face and turned back to Lily. Then, Lily looked over and called out, "Deborah!" and turned to hug me. Only then did my own mother do a double take and realize that I was the person standing next to her. I didn't know what to make of this—it was bad enough that my father hadn't recognized me but it was shocking and even more painful not to be recognized by my own mother.

I went to the cemetery with the family, then to my parents' home where everyone gathered to eat. A day or so later, I flew back to Anchorage. During the entire time I was in New York, my parents and I had no conversations about my memories; we all acted as if nothing had happened.

***

In November, about a month after the funeral, my mother called and calmly told me, "You know, I've been reading some books about incest. In all of them, the mother always knew what was going on. I wasn't aware of anything happening, so I don't think anything could have happened."

Adrenaline raced through my body. "If you don't believe anything happened, what were you doing reading books about incest?" I was fuming at her casual words.

She gave no response; she asked me no questions about why I was convinced my father had molested me or how I was feeling.

Soon after, my father called. As if presenting me with a gift, he informed me he'd seen two hypnotherapists (one session with each) and they'd concluded that nothing had happened.

I was angry. This wasn't therapy; this wasn't engaging in a process of ongoing conversations that involve analysis and reflection. How could my father expect to surface repressed memories in just two meetings with a therapist, let alone one meeting each with two therapists? I wrote my parents again.

I can no longer continue the façade that we three have been carrying on. I'm no longer willing to spare your feelings at the expense of my own well-being.

I am an incest victim and I know that to be true. Your denials will not make it any less the truth or take away the pain, the hurt or the anger.

I've spent two years trying to deal with my emotions. I've put in a lot of time and energy, not to mention money, into working through the many layers of defenses I had to build up to survive as a child and into trying to resolve my pain and anger. I don't feel that you have put in even one fraction as much effort. Dad, I am angry because you told me you would see a therapist as an act of good faith. Two hours, one hour each with a different therapist, is barely enough time to discuss your name, age and address. It is mere lip service. I'm furious because it was my understanding that you would continue in therapy so that the next time I came to New York you would have had time to do a lot of work.

Each time I have come back to New York has left me totally emotionally drained. I have tried so hard to give you time, to be empathetic, to show you that I am not trying to throw blame, shame or hatred at you.

Mom, instead of empathizing with me and trying to see the pain and the hurt that I've experienced, you asked me to try to understand what a difficult position I have put Dad in. As your daughter, I deserve your empathy. I am angry and saddened that instead of receiving motherly comfort and nurturance from you, you asked me to take care of my father. I am no longer willing to be strong for the three of us. I have done it for too long.

Mom, I feel you were not there for me when I needed you most. I needed you to hold me in your arms and tell me that it would be all right, that it was not my fault, that I would be protected and that you loved me. I needed you to take away the terror, fear and confusion caused by being faced with an adult situation at an age when I couldn't even verbalize yet. Instead of protection, comfort and nurturance, I felt shame, blame and indifference. I have been carrying this shame and guilt that don't belong to me for too many years and I am no longer willing to accept them.

I am also no longer willing to hold in the rage that belongs to both of you – I am no longer going to turn it on myself and be depressed, feel worthless, hopeless and suicidal.

I am no longer willing to carry on a superficial relationship based on pretense. In order for us to continue with any kind of relationship at all, I need honest and open communication from you. I don't see how this could be possible unless the two of you go into long term therapy with an open mind.

Based on this letter, I must have gone back to New York again before or after the funeral but don't remember a second trip. I wrote this letter as an attempt to share with my parents how painful it had been to deal with the feelings and emotions I'd been experiencing ever since I started therapy. Reading it now, it sounds like an "either you're with me or you're against me" tone. What was underneath it, however, was pure pain. My parents' failure to validate my reality left me feeling "wrong." Damaged to the core, responsible for what happened, worthless and/or crazy. I felt their acknowledgement was critical to my being able to heal.

***

In December of 1983, I began work as an Assistant Attorney General. I represented a variety of state agencies, though most of my work was on behalf of the Department of Family and Youth Services (DFYS) prosecuting cases of neglect and child abuse in Anchorage Family Court. My clients were social workers who, as representatives of DFYS, requested such things as: removing a child from the home, removing a parent from the home, having the court order family counseling, or terminating parental rights. My role was to advocate for whatever plan the social workers recommended. In cases that involved criminal actions, district attorneys prosecuted a parallel case in Criminal Court. In those cases, alleged perpetrators usually agreed to a settlement of some kind pending the criminal case, negating the need to go to trial in Family Court. In cases of sexual abuse, the perpetrators were always fathers and stepfathers and the victims were all girls. The settlement usually involved either the daughter being placed in foster care or the father/stepfather being ordered from the home.

Typically, I met with the parties involved in a conference room down the hall from the courtroom to reach a settlement prior to the hearing scheduled in Family Court. I rarely saw the children and the meetings were short. I was able to compartmentalize my feelings, so settling these cases didn't evoke strong emotions.

On a few occasions, however, it was hard to pretend that I had no personal knowledge of the impact that sexual abuse had on these girls. I believed the system in Alaska created a barrier to mothers supporting their daughters, and fathers taking responsibility. At the time, Alaska had a mandatory seven-year jail sentence for adults convicted of sexual abuse. Consequently, for a woman to support her daughter, it meant losing the man in her life, who was often the breadwinner as well. If a father took responsibility, and confirmed his daughter's claims, it meant he'd automatically go to jail for seven years, making admissions from fathers almost impossible.

Healing injuries caused by incest requires bringing the hidden family secret into the light and having the shame, guilt and responsibility taken off the child's shoulders and placed where they belong, on those of the adult perpetrator. All I wanted from my father was validation, I was angry that the law in Alaska made that highly unlikely for the girls who had been sexually abused by their fathers.

***

After sending the angry letter to my parents, our calls consisted of small talk, mostly my mother's; she shared a laundry list of activities: movies they'd seen, books she read, friends they'd gone out to dinner with.

One day, in July of 1984, my mother wrote:

Dad and I were looking at the color slides that we have taken all during the years you and Aaron were growing up. They

Mystery of Memory

brought back memories of the experiences we had. Being away on vacation in Colorado and the Virgin Islands, your going off to camp, you on horses in different camps, pictures of Barnaby [our cat], *taking you and Aaron to school, going on demonstrations, you and Cindy* [our dog] *on Nantucket, taking pictures of the two of you, you on your birthdays. Then I look at the long and thoughtful letters you used to send us when you were in Japan.* [I spent my junior year of college in Japan]

Things have changed over the years and maybe they did a little at a time, but all of a sudden it is very different. When you were away before in the past, our phone calls and letters, when you wrote, were very warm and feeling. But when I talk to you on the phone now, you are so distant that it is painful. When I mentioned your coming back for a visit, you expressed no interest. You seem to be cutting us off, but I hope this is only my reaction and not your intention.

I didn't know whether to write you about this or not. Dad feels especially helpless and doesn't know what else to do. When he wrote to you originally, he tried to offer reassurance by stating unequivocally that he had never taken any action of the sort you describe. He thinks now that this may have had just the opposite effect he had intended. He simply has no recollection of anything like that. He even subjected himself to hypnosis in an attempt to dig anything out. But that is something else.

At any rate, I'm writing to you to see if it will help to make a little dent in the problem that we have only recently become aware of. When you were home last, you greeted Dad and me warmly and affectionately. But since then, you seem to be cool and withdrawn.

I am trying to think how I would act if I were in your place. Maybe you can try to think how you would feel in my place.

I have the feeling you would never call us if we did not call you first. I hope you will agree to try to work something out with

47

at least the two of us. At best, maybe something will happen if we both try. At the worst, you can simply ignore this letter.

I hope we can do something. We both love you very much and miss you.

I was hurt and angry when I received this letter. Continuing to be in a relationship with them, however stilted, had taken a huge effort. It required me to stuff my feelings and pretend that there was nothing we needed to discuss. In my view, our family was dysfunctional and I was the only one willing to face it. At this point, I cut off communication with them, and reached out to other family members for support.

In October of 1984, I wrote to my brother Aaron and my aunt Joan, letting each of them know I was writing to the other. To my brother I wrote:

What I am writing to you about may come as a total shock to you. As you know, things have not been going well between Mom and Dad and I. There is a reason for this that I feel you should know.

I began to see a therapist in about January of 1981 because I had become so depressed I spent one solid week doing nothing but crying without being able to tell myself why. Through therapy, I have determined that I am an incest victim, that Dad sexually molested me when I was a child.

Since entering therapy and dealing with the issue of incest, my depression has been alleviated. I have also come to understand a great deal of things that had been confusing me for years. All of a sudden, pieces of my life began to fall into place and make sense. In the last few years, I have been happier and more content with myself than I have ever been before. For too many years I had been feeling guilt (for what was not my responsibility) and anger (which I had turned in on myself in the form of depression).

Mom and Dad have been aware of my knowledge for almost two years. They have alternatively denied the validity of my claim and acknowledged the possibility that it could be the truth.

I have cut off communication with them.

Mystery of Memory

Aaron, I am writing to you because I am no longer willing to keep the secret. It has made me miserable for years and has also been keeping me from having a real relationship with you—one based on openness and honesty rather than on false pretenses. I have not been able to feel close to you recently because I have been hiding so much from you. I am no longer willing to protect Dad at the expense of our relationship.

The last two times I was in New York were especially difficult for me. I felt you were critical of my decision not to stay with Mom and Dad. That hurt me a great deal because I needed your support yet did not feel I could talk to you about the reason behind my decision.

Aaron, I want to open up real communication between us. I would be very happy if I could have your support in what has been a long and very painful struggle for me.

I wrote Joan a similar letter.

Joan, you have asked me what's going on between my parents and myself that has resulted in our no longer communicating. I am writing now to tell you but first I want to say that what I need most from you now is your support. I have been afraid to talk to you about this issue because I feared your rejection. I am no longer willing to keep this family secret and feel ready to talk to you about it.

I am an incest victim. My father sexually molested me when I was a child. I confronted my parents with this fact about two years ago. They have chosen to call me a liar.

My aunt responded immediately. The first words out of her mouth after I picked up the phone were, "I always knew he was a motherfucker."

I felt validated by my aunt's response, but then she went on, "You know, when you were a little girl, there was something flirtatious about your relationship with your father."

Those words hurt; they played into my feelings of being at fault. Did she think I was in any way responsible? I had no idea how to respond. I saw nothing about my relationship with my father that even resembled flirtation.

I didn't hear from Aaron for a while. I assumed he did not believe me, and that hurt. Weeks later, he called. He told me he hadn't called earlier because he didn't know what to say, but that we should talk more the next time I came to New York. I believed my brother when he told me he didn't know what to say. At least he wasn't denying my reality as our parents were.

It may seem strange that I was so sure that I had been molested with what looks like so little evidence on which to base my conclusion: a hallucination-like vision and two flimsy memories. My data wasn't in the form of witnesses or clear and abundant memories. It was in the form of feelings and sensations that nothing else could explain: my feelings of betrayal and violation by my father, shame and worthlessness, fear of being powerless and the strange physical sensations I experienced.

The Acknowledgment

I remained out of touch with my parents until the fall of 1985. I was still living in Anchorage and working at the Attorney General's Office. I planned a trip back to New York for my brother Aaron's wedding to Sarah. At some point, my parents and I agreed to meet with a neutral therapist; we arranged to have two appointments, one with my father and me and the other with all three of us. I hoped we could reach some kind of resolution.

Before meeting with my parents, I met with my aunt and my brother for the first time since our brief phone calls after my letters. Joan was supportive and had no difficulty believing my father molested me. She shared with me her own difficulties in her relationship with my mother, who she experienced as cold, distant and at times uncaring. But this was the only conversation we had about what happened.

I went to see my brother at the Manhattan media company where he worked as a video editor. It had been about a year since we last saw each other. Like my father, my brother is almost six feet tall. Like me, he's pale and has blue-gray eyes. His dirty blond hair was cut short. He met me at the front desk and brought me to a studio in the back where we could talk privately. The room was filled with video recording and editing machinery. He sat on a stool with his back to the windows that overlooked the street. I sat on a chair facing him.

The first thing he said was, "I have a question for you. Why do you always date black men?"

I sat there in complete shock, but I wasn't angry. At least he wasn't saying he didn't believe me. I explained that I felt safer with men who in no way reminded me of my father.

***

My brother's wedding was lovely and I enjoyed seeing family and friends. The ceremony and reception were both in my parents' home.

I stayed in New York after the wedding, this time with my maternal grandmother, to meet with my parents and the therapist. At the first appointment, I met my father in the waiting room of the therapist's office. The therapist sat at a long wooden desk in the far corner of the room, my father and I on couches across from each other.

Turning to me, the therapist said, "Maybe you can share what you remember with your father and tell him how it has impacted you."

"During my second year of law school, I became deeply depressed, but had no explanation for it. As you know, I went to see Pierre. Then, about a week or so later, I had what you might call a vision." I told them about my trance-like state, of seeing my twelve-year-old self in tears, my younger self telling my adult self, 'Daddy raped me.'

"The next morning when I woke up, my depression had lifted and it felt like a burden had been taken off my shoulders. When I went back to see the therapist, Pierre, I had difficulty recalling much about my childhood, let alone anything that would explain my depression or the vision. That's why I asked for the family photo albums—to see if they would spark any memories. When I couldn't come up with anything, Pierre suggested hypnosis.

"He hypnotized me twice. The first time, I had a memory of being in the apartment we lived in on Columbia Heights. I was about a year and a half old. I was feeling lonely and wanted a hug, so I approached you and climbed into your lap. I have the sense that I didn't get any warmth from Mom; you were the affectionate one. But it seemed like there were conditions attached. At that point, you fondled my vagina. After retrieving that memory, I felt unclean, ashamed and at fault. Those feelings felt familiar.

"In the second memory, I was twelve years old. You and I were in my room and I was saying, 'No!' and you grabbed my ankles and dragged me around the room. It was terrifying.

"In addition, I had a strange experience with a seven-foot-tall man. We never had sex, but slept in the same bed one night. I woke up in the middle of the night and when I saw this man in my bed, I felt tiny, vulnerable and frightened. There was something familiar about how I felt." Then I told my father and the therapist about the time I'd felt like an infant, struggling to breathe.

"I realize I've suffered from depression most of my adult life. I used to think it was just sadness but looking back I understand that it was depression because I also felt worthless. These episodes always took place when I didn't have a boyfriend. As soon as I started seeing someone, the depression lifted. But I had never experienced depression as severe as I did before I sought out therapy. I believe having a man in my life unconsciously allowed me to feel safe and protected. And being with Miguel in the most stable, healthy relationship I'd ever been in, enabled me to feel safe enough for the memories to surface."

My father sat quietly and listened with his forehead furrowed and his lips in a straight line. I had difficulty looking at him. I focused on the therapist sitting behind his desk. My father made no attempt to interrupt me, deny what I was saying or explain or defend himself in any way. I felt heard, relieved and cleansed.

When the appointment was over, my father and I stepped out into the reception area. We were alone, surrounded by empty chairs; he broke down in tears. "Deb, I have no memory of this, but based on what you and the two therapists said, I must have done something and I am sorry."

This was all I wanted. I had a physical sense of release. Something loosened and opened up inside me. It felt like I had been one of those sponges that when you buy them are flat, dry and rigid, but when you put them in water, they open up and expand. Looking back now, perhaps my father's words were more intended as appeasement than acknowledgment. But the physical relief that came from his words constituted acknowledgment for me.

Seeing my father in tears, my heart constricted. My goal was never to hurt him or make him feel bad; particularly since I believed he had no memory of what he'd done. I just needed to know I wasn't crazy. The only thing that could explain the feelings and sensations I had been experiencing for years was my father having molested me.

I felt an immediate need to stop my father from feeling any pain so I hugged him and said, "It's OK." I felt complete. It didn't even occur to me to use this as an opportunity to talk with him further.

Later that same week we met with the therapist again, this time with my mother as well. Perhaps I used the word "betrayal" or "violation" or maybe I just expressed anger toward my father. My mother leaned forward with her eyes narrowed and burst out in his defense. My father, beside her on the couch, remained quiet, almost meek. Both my mother's intense reaction and my father's timid demeanor were unprecedented. Looking back, I wonder if my father had shared with my mother the statement he had made to me earlier that week acknowledging that he must have done something.

I responded with equal energy, my body tense as we yelled at each other. Just when the anger and energy reached its zenith, the therapist interrupted—our time was up. Then, we all walked out of the office calmly.

***

From my work in Anchorage, I knew this pattern of mothers not supporting their daughters wasn't the exception; it was the norm. Day after day, in court conference rooms sparsely furnished with a small table and chairs, I saw mothers at their husbands' sides, backing them up in the face of their daughters' accusations.

I encountered my first and only case of a mother supporting her children when the young wife of an Army service member reported that her husband had fondled and performed oral sex on her two daughters who were between three and seven. Without her husband present, she sat across the table from me. She was Latina and her English wasn't fluent. Sitting up straight in her chair, she seemed intimidated by the formality of the surroundings and anguished over what had happened to her young daughters. Her eyes remained watery throughout our conversation.

Tears came to my eyes as I told her how special she was. I shared with her that I hadn't seen any other mother support her daughter the way she was doing and told her how brave and wonderful that was. I was devastated when a few weeks later she came to a follow-up hearing and recanted. She claimed she made the story up because she had a fight with her husband. I discovered that between the first hearing and the second she realized that if her husband went to jail, she couldn't remain on base in Army housing or receive her husband's salary.

***

The same week I met with my parents in the therapist's office, my father made a second acknowledgment of sorts. I met him for lunch in Manhattan. We were in a restaurant in Tribeca, seated at a wooden table near a window looking at the menus. I felt I had achieved the closure I had been longing for, so I had no intention of bringing up the topic of my father having molested me. My father broke down in tears and said, "Deborah, I feel awful. Did I ruin your life?" I experienced his question as if he was asking for absolution and I was willing to give it to him.

"Daddy, you haven't ruined my life and I'm not angry at you. I just needed to talk about things so that they could be out in the open and no longer hidden. Now that you've acknowledged it, I can close the book and move on with my life." I meant what I said. Just as when I saw his tears in the psychiatrist's office, I felt the need to protect him so he wouldn't feel hurt.

***

A few days after I returned to Anchorage, my mother called me. "I've been feeling depressed and wonder if I should see a therapist."

I assumed her feelings were the result of the molestation having been brought to the surface. "Well, I know it's been helpful for me. I'd certainly recommend it."

I Move to Japan

About a month later, in October of 1985, I moved to Kyoto to begin a fellowship from the Japanese Ministry of Education to study law in Japan for a year and a half. I had majored in East Asian Studies as an undergraduate at Harvard, spent my junior year in Japan, and wanted to go back. While I loved Alaska's natural beauty and the seemingly unending days of summer, I was ready to leave the long dark winter nights behind me.

Soon after, my parents traveled to Japan. I was edgy, tense and irritable around them. Once again, just when I thought the issue was resolved, uncomfortable feelings started to surface. It felt like there was a dead moose in the room that my parents insisted on ignoring. I became resentful. I guess I was expecting them to know what to do and how to broach the subject.

One day after I escorted my parents back to their hotel, I exploded. "You're both acting like nothing happened! Do you think we can just move on? Do you think we resolved everything in just two one-hour sessions with a therapist? Do you think we can just pretend everything is the same?"

I was hurt that they didn't feel the need to initiate a conversation and perhaps even share some remorse. I saw my outburst as a plea, making clear how hurt I was and how much I wanted them to acknowledge my pain. Now, I can see that I never directly told them I was hurting or what I wanted. With slightly stunned expressions, they looked at me as if they didn't understand. How could they? My words didn't communicate my feelings or needs clearly. Further, in New York, I had acted, and felt, as if I'd closed the book on that chapter of my life and had no need or desire to discuss it again. When we met in New York, I never asked my father what he thought had happened or what specifically led him to tell me that he'd done something. I had closed off the conversation by saying that all I needed was my father's acknowledgment. What might've happened if I hadn't let him off the hook?

III. Incest and Insanity

NUTS

In 1987, my fellowship in Japan ended and I moved to Washington, DC. I was conversationally fluent in Japanese, and hoped I'd be able to find work there using my language skills.

I lived in a small one-bedroom apartment in the DuPont Circle area. I regularly rented movies from a video store a few blocks away. One day, I watched the movie *Nuts*.

Barbara Streisand plays Claudia Draper, a high-class call girl. She killed one of her clients in self-defense and was accused of murder. Without her knowledge or consent, her parents hire an attorney for her. They want Claudia deemed incompetent to stand trial to protect them from shameful publicity about their daughter's chosen profession. Despite her vocal opposition, Claudia is sent to a mental institution for evaluation.

Seeing Claudia rendered voiceless and helpless triggered something in me. My body tensed. I experienced a deep, almost primitive sense of fear and vulnerability. It felt eerily familiar. If her parents could have her deemed insane, mine could do the same to me.

Even now, I relate to this visceral sense of powerlessness. I read about a woman who found herself awake in the middle of surgery.

Her anesthesia had been inadequate so she felt everything but was unable to alert the doctors because she had been given a muscle relaxant and couldn't move or speak. Tears streamed down my face while reading about it and I had difficulty breathing—this woman's experience of complete helplessness, in a situation in which she was supposed to have been safe and protected, flooded me with grief and fear.

***

When Claudia meets with the psychiatrist who has concluded she isn't competent to stand trial, she finds herself caught in a frightening Catch-22. She's been falsely deemed mentally incompetent but the psychiatrist cites Claudia's natural and appropriate anger as further evidence of insanity.

This brought to mind an experience I had with Kathryn, my therapist in Anchorage. We never developed a close relationship and I confronted her about it.

"I want to switch to another therapist in the collective because I don't feel you're a good fit for me. I feel no warmth from you and that leaves me feeling unsafe and unable to be open with you."

She told me I didn't feel any warmth because I was transferring my feelings about my mother onto her. She thought rather than switch therapists, it was important that I work through this transference with her. The more I argued, the more she saw my words as evidence of transference. Like the psychiatrist in *Nuts*, my therapist had the power to define reality in a way that invalidated my own. I found another therapist outside the collective.

As the movie continues, we discover that Claudia's stepfather had molested her as a child and her mother had done nothing to protect her. We see a scene in which Claudia, about ten years old, sits on her bed in her nightgown crying. Her mother, holding a drink, sees her crying but passes by, doing nothing. That brought to mind the image of my mother drinking a Martini in the kitchen while my father was dragging me around the room upstairs.

Mystery of Memory

Neither of my parents had called me insane, threatened to commit me, or denied my claims. However, my parents' behavior in Japan and since I returned to the States, led me to believe they wanted to sweep the whole thing under the rug. I thought I had been so clear in asking them to talk with me. Their apparent lack of interest felt tantamount to a denial and invalidation of my reality.

The parents in the movie, an older respectable-looking couple, reminded me of my parents; two middle-class individuals, who to the outside world were the epitome of upstanding citizens. I sensed my parents would rather see me in a mental institution than confront their own culpability. I felt scared and vulnerable—I had very little to support my claims. My vision and wispy memories, while evidence to me, would be considered proof of insanity to others.

***

After watching *Nuts*, I started to worry about being seen as crazy. This reminded me of my experience of seeing *The Exorcist*, when I was in the eleventh grade. Seeing that film had activated a deep-seated fear in me. It activated something else as well: intense shame.

When the fear persisted, my parents asked me if I wanted to see a psychiatrist and, in desperation, I agreed. I went to the appointment on my own. As soon as the psychiatrist asked me what was wrong, I broke into tears. I was unable to stop crying for the whole session.

"What are you crying about?"

"I don't know."

"Well, what do you think is the reason you're crying?"

I had no idea and couldn't tell her. She kept asking me as if I was hiding something from her. I thought she believed something was wrong with me. I experienced her as cold and her tone as accusatory, as if she was interrogating me instead of trying to understand me. By the end of the session, I was furious. She thought I was crazy. Was I?

About a week later, I was in the study and saw a letter on my father's desk. "Is that letter from the psychiatrist?"

"Yes."

"What did she say?"

"She recommended ongoing treatment."

"Well, I'm never going to see her again!"

I spoke in a forceful voice as if I was confident despite feeling vulnerable and scared. If she thought there was something wrong with me, maybe there was, but no fucking way was I going to let her treat me as if I were crazy.

Writing this book, I watched *The Exorcist* again to see if it might give me any insight. Throughout the movie, even with the bed shaking and furniture moving across rooms, no one believes the girl when she says she didn't make those things happen. The doctors see her as the source of the problem. At that point, I had an "a-ha" moment. The message from *The Exorcist* and my negative experience with the psychiatrist was clear. Nobody believes allegations by children. Add to that the message of *Nuts:* respected middle-class parents don't want their image tarnished; rather than facing an uncomfortable truth, they call you crazy.

It was only now, after re-watching both movies that I came to understand exactly what had triggered my fear and the sensation of being wrong and ashamed when I watched *The Exorcist*. Hidden in my unconscious, in the same place my repressed memories resided, was an assumption that if my reality is not believed, it means I must be wrong in the core of my being and/or crazy. Nonverbal as I may have been when my father molested me, my body knew that I was being violated. My father, the person I was supposed to feel safe with and trust, acted as if what he was doing was neither wrong nor a violation. This left me feeling I must be intrinsically bad and that I could not trust my own feelings and sense of reality.

Not being believed has greater meaning for me than the average person. Having my reality questioned can lead me to feel bad as a person, worthless and/or crazy. As a teenager, seeing the adults' reaction to the girl in *The Exorcist* seemed to confirm this unconscious assumption.

I now understood why I had overreacted in an interaction I had with a surgeon during my first year of law school. I had had an operation to repair a dislocated shoulder. In pain after the surgery, I kept asking for a heating pad or a muscle relaxant—I sensed the pain was more from stiffness than the actual incision. The nurses never brought me either. When the surgeon came to discharge me, I told him how bad the pain was.

He said, "The operation was a success. There's no reason for you to have any pain." Reviewing the chart without looking at me, he asked, "Are you worried about anything? Are you experiencing any stress at home?"

Rather than simply saying, "no," or becoming irritated, I became enraged. By doubting the reality of my pain, it felt like he was insinuating I was crazy.

Other things fell into place. This explained why I often have difficulty trusting my own feelings, particularly when it comes to betrayal or violation of any kind. My default responses are, "My feelings aren't valid," "I must be crazy to have those feelings," "There must be something wrong and worthless about me for having those feelings," or "Whatever happened must be my fault." Instead of feeling betrayed, I often feel worthless and responsible for whatever happened.

***

I was lonely and miserable in DC. I didn't know many people and hated the politics of the town, so in 1988 I moved back to New York. Until I found a job and was able to afford my own place, I had to stay for a few months with my parents. I hated being dependent on them.

As in Japan, we avoided the topic of the molestation. Staying in their home, I felt too vulnerable to bring up the subject. Fortunately, I got a job soon as an NYC Assistant Corporation Counsel, and found a place to live in the Prospect Heights section of Brooklyn.

Around that time, I had a strange interaction with my sister-in-law, Sarah. We hadn't spent much time together. All I knew about her was that she had worked for a bank and had an African violet collection. She invited me over to lunch so we could spend time together alone.

We ate in the dining room, making small talk about the food and living in Brooklyn. Out of the blue, Sarah asked, "If Aaron and I have children, would you worry about leaving them with him?"

Evidently my brother had shared my letter. When she said, "him," I assumed she meant my father. "As long as my mother is there, I wouldn't worry about it, but I wouldn't leave children alone with him."

Then, to my surprise, I realized she was talking about my brother.

I told her it was possible that my father had molested my brother as well. That I'd done significant reading about incest over the years, and that incest can repeat itself from one generation to the next. It was worth thinking about, I told her.

I don't remember the context, but later in the conversation she said, "I'm like your mother; I tend to turn my emotions into Martinis."

Once again, I saw the image of my mother drinking a Martini in the kitchen. Sarah saying that seemed like more than a coincidence.

***

During that time, I attended family gatherings and visited my parents every few weekends, typically for brunch. I'd enter the apartment, step into the vestibule and hang up my coat and purse. Then I'd walk into the dining room, where they'd be reading the New York Times. My father would be at the head of the table, my mother seated to his right. They'd look up as I came in and one of them would ask, "So how are you doing?"

"Fine." I'd reply and take the seat to my father's left, directly across from my mother. My father would then tell me about an article he'd just read or a book he was reading.

"Hmm, tell me more." I tried my best to sound interested despite the tightness in my chest. My body was vigilant and on guard the entire time I was with them. I limited conversation to the superficial and general; I was anxious to leave at the first possible moment. Once I had been there long enough not to be rude, I'd excuse myself. As their apartment door closed behind me, the tension left my body and I felt light and free.

My feeling that I was only safe and protected when I had a man in my life persisted. My experience visiting my parents was completely different when I brought along George, the man I was seeing. I had spoken with him about my memories and his response was empathetic. Sitting down for brunch, my breathing was normal and I wasn't on the edge of my seat ready for an opportunity to leave. With a man beside me, I was able to relax and let my guard down. I felt protected.

I had still not recovered any additional memories so I started working with Ruth, a therapist in New York. I remember how excited I was returning from my first session with her. I wrote in my journal, "Today I am joining with Ruth to explore my past and find the memories I've been seeking." I thought it was just a matter of time before I would unearth additional memories. I was wrong.

***

My relationship with George was short-lived. It turned out he was living with someone. In the period before I found another boyfriend, I didn't want to spend a lot of time with my family. Nonetheless, I continued to visit. In November of 1988, however, I declined an invitation to dinner at my brother's house. I just didn't have the energy to face my parents and the rest of the family on my own. I never reached out to my brother or my aunt Joan, or shared with my parents how uncomfortable I was around them; I felt too vulnerable.

Shortly thereafter, Sarah invited me to dinner. We met at a Thai restaurant on Flatbush Avenue, walking distance from both our homes. We ordered and chatted. While we ate, she informed me, "The family is anxious about you and felt that someone should talk to you."

"Why?"

"Well, everyone is worried that you're depressed and your mother is concerned about the quality of men you're involved with; she doesn't feel that they're your equals."

I was baffled. I didn't say much in response at dinner. Later that evening, I called my childhood friend Laura to vent. "You're never going to believe what my mother did. She told my sister-in-law to tell me that she was concerned about the quality of men I'm involved with. Can you believe that?"

After a short pause, she said haltingly, "Deb...I feel awful...I didn't tell you, but your mother called me a week or so ago. She said she was worried that you are always dating black men."

Why would my mother, a supporter of racial justice, have said something like this? When my sister-in-law used the words, "the quality of men" I was dating, I assumed it was because they were not professionals. My Columbian boyfriend in Alaska was a real estate agent, and George, a black man, worked as a personal trainer.

My mother had raised the issue of the ethnicity of my friends once when I was in college. Home for a school break, I told my mother about a female friend of mine from school and she asked, "What is she?"

"What do you mean, 'What is she?'" I asked.

"Is she black or white or...?"

"What difference does the color of my friends make? Do you ask Aaron the color of his friends? It doesn't matter if they're white or black or purple. The only thing you should be asking me is if they're good friends or not." Without waiting for a response, I walked out of the room.

My mother's questions at that time demonstrated a double standard, but this was blatant hypocrisy. I was livid. Not only could I not understand my mother's concern, but wondered why no one in my family was willing to talk with me directly. My family had always communicated indirectly, but this was unbelievable. Perhaps my parents thought I'd see Sarah as a neutral party. All I saw was cowardice on their part. What was worse, suddenly I had become the black sheep of the family. This set off my fear of being seen as crazy. All my relatives who knew about my memories would rather see something wrong with me than reflect on the possibility of dysfunction in the family.

I wrote an angry letter to my mother.

I am writing to you because I am furious. Where does this family get the right to hold a summit meeting to discuss "Deborah's Depression?" The issue isn't that Deborah is depressed. The issue is that Deborah is ambivalent about spending time with her family. That's why I haven't been coming to see you frequently. This family has issues that have been left unresolved. These issues were dealt with once, before I left for Japan, in a very superficial manner and never since. That is not how problems are resolved.

I am furious that even if you did believe that I was depressed and were concerned about it, you didn't have the courage to talk to me directly. Since when do families elect ambassadors to engage in communication for them? I am through with this family's modus operandi of no one ever talking directly to anyone. That's half the problem right there. When it comes to problems in our family, people either act like an ostrich and stick their heads in the sand as if they don't exist, or they deal with the problem through an intermediary rather than directly. In this case, you have done both. As to the issue, which is the real problem, the incest, you have acted like ostriches and chosen not to deal with it. Rather, you pretend the problem is my depression and you send an ambassador to talk to me about it. Well, the embassy in my house is no longer open for business. I do not deal in indirect communications anymore.

What is worst about your 'concern' is your obsession with what color the friends in my life are. What the hell difference does or should that make? If you are so concerned, why don't you ask the questions that should be important to a caring parent? Are Deborah's friends supportive of her, do they make her happy, do they bring joy to her life? All you ask is what color they are.

Where were you when I was being molested? Where were you then when you should have stopped it and protected me? Your concern now is too little, too late and totally unnecessary. Look at your own house before you start to find problems in mine.

Looking at this letter now, as with my other letter, all I see is anger. But there was an incredible amount of pain underneath. I didn't feel safe enough to express my hurt in a vulnerable and open way. Nonetheless, I thought I was conveying it in my letter. That made it even more difficult to understand why my parents didn't reach out.

I Hit a Wall: My Father Recants

After I sent the letter, my parents and I were in and out of communication. In 1991, I started dating Jeffrey, a locksmith who owned his own business. He was a black man of average height, kept his hair cut short and usually wore a uniform and construction boots. We first met when he repaired the intercom system in my apartment building. It was summer and he had to keep running up and down stairs, testing the intercoms in all the apartments. I offered him a cold drink and we talked a bit.

Jeffrey's shop was just blocks from where I lived so we saw each other on the street frequently after that. Once, I needed to have him change the locks on my front door and offered him a beer when he was done. We sat together in my kitchen chatting. The next time I saw him on the street, he made reference to something I had told him about my job; I was impressed that he had listened so well. After a couple of years greeting each other on the street, we started going out. During one of the periods that my parents and I were in communication, Jeffrey and my parents met. Despite my mother's earlier concerns about my dating black men, my parents liked Jeffrey and got along well with him. Even when my parents and I were estranged, they called him whenever they needed a locksmith and always treated him with affection.

Shortly after Jeffrey and I started dating, I left the practice of law and became the Director of the Career Services Department at New York Law School. I headed a staff of eight, providing students and alumni with career counseling, job search-related workshops and educational panels, and administering recruitment and job development programs. During this time, I became involved in a number of projects to help graduates of color and first-generation law school graduates gain access to and succeed in the legal profession.

***

Since sending the angry letter to my mother in 1988, I had tried every way I could to get my parents to talk with me instead of pretending that there was nothing to talk about. I felt sure that if I just found the right approach, my parents would open up and we could find resolution.

Among my numerous efforts was to give them a copy of a documentary about child abuse, *Scared Silent: Exposing and Ending Child Abuse*. The film had aired as an Oprah Winfrey special in 1992 and told three stories of sexual abuse, physical abuse, and emotional abuse. The documentary was meant to provide support and direction in discussing child abuse. I thought it might be a way to break the ice. They agreed to watch it.

Bringing *Scared Silent* to my parents didn't have the result I hoped for. I went to their house a week or two after giving them the video. It was early afternoon and the dining room was well lit with natural light. I sat on the long side of the rectangular table. My father sat to my left at the end of the table; my mother sat on his left side. I tried to begin a discussion about the film and what it brought up for them.

"So, what were your thoughts about the film?"

"We don't know what to tell you," my father said.

"You don't have anything to say about the video?"

"No, because nothing ever happened."

I was dumbfounded. The last thing I expected my father to do was recant the acknowledgements he had made years earlier. "What about the times when you acknowledged that something had happened?" I asked.

"I only said that because you blackmailed us. You said you would refuse to communicate with us if I didn't say that," he replied.

I couldn't believe that after all these years he not only denied that anything happened, but accused me of blackmailing him. "So if nothing happened, why did Mom get depressed after we met with the therapist?"

"Depression runs in the women in this family," he responded. His tone made it sound as if the women in the family were defective. As if we were all crazy and damaged while he was blameless. My fear about my parents preferring to see me as crazy rather than acknowledge what happened felt more real than ever.

During the entire conversation, my mother, a strong, intelligent woman, didn't contribute a word. She sat hunched in her chair, and maintained her silence. How could she just sit there and let my father talk that way about the "women in this family?"

"You're calling the women in this family crazy?" I yelled. "There's nothing wrong with you?"

Leaning forward with his eyes narrowed and his right eyebrow raised, my father yelled back. I don't remember what he said but I recall the rage in his face and the intensity of his anger.

This time I wasn't frightened. I was furious; my upper body and hands shook from the adrenaline that rushed through me. I felt my chest tighten, as if a firm wall came down covering and protecting my heart. I felt strong.

He looked as if he was on the verge of hitting me. I knew I was never going to let this man hurt me again. I leaned forward, egging him on. "So, are you gonna hit me?"

He sat back in his chair. I got up from the table, walked to the door, closed it behind me, and left. The shaking lasted for a long while after.

My worst nightmare had come true. My father chose to call me crazy rather than admit his guilt.

***

Writing this book decades later, I found *Scared Silent* online and watched it again. In the first part, Eva, a young woman, with short straight blond hair, speaks about her father molesting her. Her words hit me in my gut. "I felt really alone. So when someone gave me attention, that is, my Dad, it was sort of attention that I needed and was missing." When I climbed into my father's lap as a toddler, that's what I wanted, just some warmth and attention.

Eva's father, a chubby-faced middle-aged white man with glasses, shared, "Part of the grooming for this is to indicate that—you know—you can't tell anybody about this because they'll come in and break up the family."

When I heard those words, what came to mind was a childhood nightmare I had when I was six or seven years old. In the dream, my parents had gotten divorced and my mother was married to and living with a Chinese man. I met her in the lobby of the apartment building we lived in. It was dark. I went to her and cried and cried, and begged her to please come back home. Despite my crying, my mother simply told me she couldn't.

I woke from the nightmare crying. Then, I saw next to my bed what looked like a throne and a man dressed as an Egyptian pharaoh, regal in a large headpiece and robes. As he sat there, he put his finger to his lips, telling me it wasn't safe to talk.

***

In *Scared Silent,* we learn that Eva's mother was sexually molested as a child herself. Because she was unable to face the pain of her own abuse, she shut out signs of her daughter's abuse, such as Eva's sadness as a child. I thought about my mother telling me that I was depressed when I was six years old.

I didn't see my mother as a place of support, solace or protection. In junior high school, I recall feeling suicidal and considering suffocating myself with a pillow as I cried myself to sleep. It never occurred to me to talk with either of my parents. I called out in my head to my maternal grandmother. Even though we weren't close enough for her to be someone I would reach out to, I just needed to think someone was out there.

It turns out that when Eva's father was six years old, a neighbor had sexually abused him. He explained that because he came from a strict religious family, he had no way of telling anyone what happened. He learned to protect himself by taking control of his life and everyone around him. His need to always be in control reminded me of my father.

***

Eva's father went to jail and into treatment. After his release, they met. Part way through their meeting, Eva's father started to cry. Her response was, "I see you being very vulnerable and my first reaction would be to want to take care of you and make sure you didn't hurt and that's exactly what I've done all my life and I don't want to do that."

Seeing Eva respond that way, I wish I hadn't been so quick to protect my father when he apologized to me.

Even though the next part of the program was about children who had been physically abused, I decided to watch it anyway. Jill, a middle-aged white woman with short brown hair, bangs and glasses, shared that her father physically abused her when she was a child. She then spoke about a time her son had colic and wouldn't stop crying. She was exhausted and wanted to take a nap, so she "put him in his carriage in the basement and stuffed a cloth in his mouth to keep him quiet." That brought to mind my father putting a pillow over my face when I was an infant and wouldn't stop crying.

***

The first child I parented was Jeffrey's five-year-old son, Omar. When Jeffrey and I first started dating, Omar lived with his paternal grandmother. Jeffrey and Omar's mother alternated custody of Omar on weekends, but Jeffrey's mother planned to leave the U.S. and return to Barbados. So, Jeffrey fought for and gained legal and physical custody of Omar. I never wanted children, but I found myself suddenly in the role of stepmother, completely unprepared.

If I was going to be a parent, I was going to do it right. I went to Borders Books, found the Parenting Section and spent a good half hour perusing the books. I bought *How to Talk So Kids Will Listen & Listen So Kids Will Talk* and tried to get Jeffrey to read it with me, but he had no interest. Jeffrey worked on Saturdays so on the weekends when Omar stayed with us, I was left to take care of him. I felt overwhelmed and tried to talk with Jeffrey about it. He got angry and accused me of not wanting Omar in my life.

I put incredible pressure on myself to be a good parent. I made sure we found things to do on Sundays that Omar would enjoy. We went to places like the Bronx Zoo and the Intrepid Sea Air & Space Museum. I thought I was supposed to keep Omar amused and occupied at all times. Simply playing was something I didn't know how to do so I felt like a failure as a parent. I was enormously relieved therefore when a friend of mine, a parent of three children, informed me that there was nothing wrong with telling a child to go play by him/herself. That hadn't occurred to me as an option.

***

In the spring of 1993, about a year after my father recanted, Jeffrey, seven-year-old Omar and I, went to the Brooklyn Botanic Gardens. We were in the Japanese Garden strolling along a path surrounding a pond filled with huge koi. The path winds around the water and crosses a small, wooden bridge. I walked a bit ahead of Jeffrey and Omar and saw my mother. She stood on the bridge, feeding bread to the fish with my nephew, Michael. I hadn't seen my nephew since his *bris*; even though Aaron and I never had a specific falling out, we were no longer in contact after I broke off communication with my parents. Michael was about one and a half, and looked like my brother did when he was that age.

I approached them on the bridge. Michael was between my mother and me. I waited until she looked up. "This must be Michael." I said.

She looked at me, but didn't respond. It was as if she didn't recognize me, but smiled to be polite and turned her attention back to Michael. I was shocked. This was similar to what had happened at the funeral home. How did my own mother not know who I was? A wall of anger came over me. Fuck her! I was speechless and walked off infuriated.

When Jeffrey and Omar reached the bridge, she recognized them at once and only then realized that I was the woman who just spoke to her. She called out my name, but I ignored her.

I Begin to Question My Reality

My father recanting left me questioning my own sense of reality. I bounced back and forth between anger and self-doubt.

A voice inside asked, "Why haven't you recovered any more memories of being molested? Isn't there supposed to be an instant in which memories came flooding back?" I had no witnesses—only my vision and memory fragments. This self-doubt was agonizing and I spiraled into depression, feeling worthless and crazy.

The pain of having my reality invalidated resulted in the angriest moment in my life. Later that year, Jeffrey cheated on me.

When I needed to reach Jeffrey while he was working, I called his store and left messages with Janet, his cashier. On numerous occasions, he said he didn't receive them. I complained that he needed to speak with Janet about conveying my messages; he simply told me not to call the store any more, to contact him through his beeper.

My instincts told me he was cheating. I asked him point blank if he was sleeping with someone else, and he denied it. He made excuses and insinuated that something was wrong with me to even consider that. He denied sleeping with anyone else and said he loved me and that I must be crazy to think he was cheating on me. I began to doubt my feelings.

When the phone call came, I knew it was true.

"You must be the only one on Vanderbilt Avenue who doesn't know your boyfriend is sleeping with the bitch who works in his store." Pretending to be a stranger, it was Janet herself who called me.

I was angry that he had cheated, but I was livid because he had made me doubt my own intuition. My anger was like nothing I experienced before. Energy surged from my gut, moved up into my chest, radiated throughout my body and beyond.

Jeffrey called. "Please Deb, let me come over. I'm sorry—just let me come over and talk to you."

"You don't want to come over here because I will tear you limb from limb! You're a piece of shit, you motherfucker!"

My voice came from the depths of my abdomen to above my rib cage and then rushed out of my mouth. I yelled loud enough that I'm sure half the building heard me. I didn't care.

The next day, my throat was so raw I couldn't talk. I felt proud of myself. I had taken charge. He would never come back into my life. He could beg and plead and I'd never take him back.

With Jeffrey, my reality was corroborated, but now that my father had recanted, the burden of proof rested on me to prove what was impossible for me to substantiate. I tortured myself with doubt because I didn't have anything that others would consider to be evidence. My internal reality—my feelings, sensations, and beliefs —meant nothing to anyone else.

I Reach Out Again

In the summer of 1993 shortly after I broke up with Jeffrey, alone at the Angelika movie theatre in Lower Manhattan, I saw my parents in line ahead of me. Unsure, I took a breath and walked over to where they were standing. I gave each of them a hug, saying, "Hi." After an awkward moment, I asked, "So what movie are you here to see?"

"We're seeing *The Wedding Banquet.*"

"Oh, me too." Without more discussion, we handed over our tickets, walked into the theatre and sat down to watch the movie together.

The movie is about Wei Tong, a Chinese-American gay man living in New York City, in a committed relationship with his live-in lover, Simon. Wei Tong's Taiwanese parents don't know he's gay. Unable to confront them with the truth, he agrees to marry Wei-Wei, an immigrant from China who needs a green card. When his parents receive the announcement, they insist on coming to New York for the wedding. The deception continues until Wei Tong's secret comes out and to his surprise, both his parents embrace his relationship with Simon.

The film ended and we parted ways. I dared to hope the movie could be an opening for my parents to consider how secrets had impacted our family and I fantasized that they'd call me in a few days to talk, but they didn't.

***

A few weeks later, after hearing nothing, I wrote them a letter.

I am glad that we were able to spend some time together the other day when we met accidentally at the movies. I have given much thought since then to the idea of re-establishing contact with the two of you. Unfortunately, I have concluded that I will be unable to spend time with you in the near future.

Perhaps you will be better able to understand how I feel when you look back in time. It has been eleven years since I confronted the two of you with my memories. For eleven years, I have tried everything in my power to make a relationship with the two of you work. To the extent that we have had a relationship, it has continued at my expense and well-being.

I feel that I am the only one who has made efforts to improve our relationship by telling you how I feel in person and in writing. I have tried to explain to you the issues that interfere with our having a healthy relationship. I have bared my soul to you. I have made overture after overture after overture to no avail and without receiving any more understanding on your part of my feelings.

During the past few months, neither of you has even bothered to take the time to put your thoughts and feelings into writing to indicate any kind of soul searching on your part, any recognition, understanding or appreciation of who I am or what growing up was like for me.

In your lack of action, you have made a choice—and I acknowledge that it is yours to make. You have chosen to try to continue our relationship by pretending that there is no problem and at times to actively deny that there is/was one. I am no longer going to try to make you change your mind about this choice you have made.

Maybe in time I will be able to have a relationship with the two of you without feeling hurt in the process. For this to be possible, I need to resolve on my own issues that I had hoped I would have your assistance in resolving.

This decision is not about blame or threats. It is about reality. I am not asking you to do anything or say anything. I am merely explaining to you that as things are now, I am unable to spend time with you.

Yet again, in my pain, I couldn't see that this letter wasn't likely to get me what I was so desperately seeking.

In response, I received a typewritten note.

We recognize that you are deeply unhappy because of things that happened in the past. We wish we could do something to change the past. But we can't.

We want you to know that we love you and care about you very much. Please know that we are here for you whenever you want or need us.

I knew my father had written the letter. My mother rarely used the typewriter.

***

Jeffrey and I were apart for about a year. That entire time, I mourned the loss of our relationship. Despite his lies, I felt as if I'd never find anyone else to love and accept me. When I told him about being molested, he had believed and comforted me. I would lay across him, my ribs against his ribs, my head turned to the side feeling the warmth of the skin of his chest. His long arms encircled me and I felt safe and loved. He was the only one. Without someone to love me, I was worthless. We got back together in 1994.

***

One day in 1994, I woke up feeling concerned for my nephew Michael. I hadn't seen him since I briefly ran into him and my mother in the Botanic Gardens. I had no idea why, but I felt anxious and frightened on his behalf. I realized he was slightly older than I was when my father molested me and felt he might be in danger of being molested as well.

I decided to write a letter to my sister-in-law expressing my concerns for his safety. I made no accusations. I expressed my fears.

In response, she wrote that she was sure that my brother had not been molested and she doubted that I was either. Her letter felt like a kick in the gut.

***

In December of 1994, Jeffrey proposed. Although we were still estranged, I wrote my parents to let them know I was going to get married. Despite my last letter, I was still unable to let go of the hope my parents would provide the validation I needed to believe myself. Since I couldn't recover more memories on my own, more than anything, I wanted external substantiation of what I was feeling inside.

I am happy to write to let you know that Jeffrey and I have become engaged although we have not yet set a date for our wedding. I am sorry to say, however, that with the way things stand now, I do not intend to invite you to the wedding.

I would like you to understand that this is not in any way meant to hurt either of you. Rather, it is because I want my wedding to be a day of happiness only, and not marred by any negative emotions that your presence will bring up for me.

I cannot begin to tell you how painful this decision is for me. The whole idea of becoming engaged and not being able to talk to family about it is hurtful. I feel like an orphan. The fact that I have no family member in my life who has tried to feel for me and my pain—that I have no family member who has attempted in any way to understand me or make amends for the pain I have experienced is unbearably hurtful. I cannot tell you how angry and hurt I am that to this day all that either of you seem capable of doing is dropping me one to two line notes. How can you so easily let go of your only daughter? How can you not have engaged in some sort of soul-searching from which you could have produced some indication of your feelings and responses to what I have been telling you for years? I have given the two of you chance after chance to meet me halfway and you have shown yourselves to be completely unable or unwilling to do so. I find this unthinkable.

To this day, every part of my life is negatively affected by the fact that I was molested and betrayed. I will not allow the beginning of a new chapter in my life to be affected negatively as well. I am starting a completely new life with a new family and leaving behind the family that cannot see or feel my pain. I hope you can at least be happy for me that I have someone like Jeffrey in my life.

Their response was again typewritten by my father.

There is no way that you will be able to appreciate the hurt of parents losing their child. Just as we have apparently never been able to fully appreciate your experience.

At our age we have much more to look back at than we have to look forward to. We remember when you and Aaron were very young that we felt you were special. Your independent spirit, your intellectual curiosity, your keen interest in social issues set you apart. You seemed so secure and confident. Which is apparently why early on when Aaron was having such problems, we were not always alert to some of your needs. For this we are deeply sorry.

We have memories of your stealing the show as the Grand Vizier at P.S. 8...giving out political leaflets on Henry Street and telling us of the people you spoke with...going to Washington for demonstrations...taking Cindy [our dog] *to camp – and also organizing the girls to win the right to work in the stables as well as in the kitchen...working with Heather to organize St. Ann's for a social action...going to Quaker meetings to find one that you preferred and later joining the synagogue...watching you in the Judo demonstration during Operation Sail down in the financial area...talking to the police when they picked you up while you were living in the streets in an experiment you persuaded us to permit after the Encampment...calling you and Aaron home from school to help Cindy give birth...reading the Autobiography of Malcolm X...taking you and Aaron on vacations to the Virgin Islands, Colorado and the beach...*

We will think of you with love and hope that somehow some day we may be able to start anew.

Of course, we send you, Jeffrey and Omar our warmest good wishes for your future happiness.

The letter sounded more like a eulogy than an attempt to rebuild our relationship. I was so hurt. I couldn't believe that they weren't taking action of some kind in response to the pain I described to them in my letter.

***

After I received their note, I called one of my mother's oldest friends, Ann. She had known me my entire life and was the closest to family I had. I called her in tears and asked her if she knew why I had not been in touch with my parents, and she said yes. I shared my version and crying, told her, "Ann, I need to feel that you're on my side because no one else in my family is."

"I'm not taking sides. I know this is painful for you. And I know your mother would love to talk with you. She's very upset about this too."

Even though Ann never specifically said she believed me, she didn't express doubt either and offered me empathy and love. I needed someone to believe me so I wouldn't doubt my own sanity.

More Invisibility

In January of 1995, Jeffrey and I got married. We realized we couldn't afford a reception in New York with a lot of guests. I was going to be in New Orleans for a business conference and we thought it would be fun to get married there. I arrived first and attended the conference events. Jeffrey joined me a few days later. We reserved a suite at one of the nicest hotels in New Orleans, the

Windsor Court Hotel, and arranged to have a judge perform the wedding there.

My best friend from Anchorage, Lewis, came with his girlfriend; he was my "matron of honor." Linda, a friend of Jeffrey's and mine, brought Omar to New Orleans the night before the wedding so he could serve as Jeffrey's best man. I invited a few work colleagues who had attended the conference. The ceremony took place in the morning and we took everyone out to brunch afterwards at Brennan's, a well-known New Orleans restaurant. We had no time or money for a honeymoon, so a few hours later we flew back to New York.

After getting married, Jeffrey and I moved to a larger apartment. We wanted to stay in Prospect Heights. We looked for weeks at apartments and houses, all either too small or too expensive. We finally found an apartment we could afford. The husband of the family who lived there had been transferred to the Midwest. They'd already moved and were anxious to sell, so they accepted our low offer. This apartment happened to be in the same building that Aaron and his family had lived in since his marriage. I was hesitant but the apartment was perfect. We didn't run across my brother or his family; our apartment was on the other side of the building.

Soon after moving in, I became pregnant with my daughter. I had come to enjoy parenting Omar and decided I'd like to have a baby after all. I wrote my parents to let them know. I was like a dog with a bone who wouldn't let go of it. I believed that if I just used the right words to let them know how much pain I was in, their response would be different. I couldn't believe they would rather lose their daughter than do whatever self-exploration was needed for them to be able to confirm my reality.

I write because I have news to give you. I am currently four months pregnant and due to have a baby in mid-August. The decision to give you this information has been a difficult one for me. Much as I wanted to share this wonderful news with you, I have hesitated. I am still in a state of disbelief at your complete lack of responsiveness to all my prior attempts at communication. Yes, I know I said I did not want to meet with you in person any more. I never said that we could not communicate in writing. Your sole communications to me have indicated a continued complete lack of understanding (or desire to understand) what life has been like for me. I have reached out to the two of you over and over and over. In response to the news of my marriage, I received a letter from you that sounded as if you were writing about a daughter who had passed away. It is so hard for me to believe that it is easier for the two of you to see me as dead than to make any attempts to try to understand me and look into yourselves. This has been a hurtful truth for me to bear. It has made it very difficult for me to want to reach out to you anymore, even if to share more news of joy.

Mom, last spring when I ran into you in the Botanic Gardens and greeted you and Michael, you didn't even recognize me. This is the second time this has happened. When I came into the funeral home at Grandpa's funeral, you didn't recognize me then either. This is incredible to me and very painful. It is just one more indication of your inability to see who I am and what I feel and have felt.

I send you this news because I feel you have a right to know that you will have another grandchild. I have no expectations about what you may or may not do with this news.

I hope you two are healthy and well.

I don't remember if they responded or not.

***

One evening, during my ninth month of pregnancy, Jeffrey and I were walking home. Around the corner from our building, we crossed paths with my parents. They passed by without greeting us and I made no attempt to greet them. I kept walking, but Jeffrey called out to them. My father turned around and nodded, but kept walking. Just as my mother had done in the Botanic Gardens, he looked at us as if we were strangers. I was furious and hurt. It didn't feel as if they had ignored me. It felt as if they hadn't recognized me.

They knew I was pregnant. They knew I lived in the same building as my brother. They knew my husband was black. How could they see an interracial couple, with an extremely pregnant woman and not at least consider that it might be their daughter and her husband?

It seemed that I was dead to them, non-existent and invisible. In my mind, they had emotionally sat *shiva* for me. In the Jewish religious tradition, when a parent, spouse, sibling or child dies, the immediate family members sit *shiva*. For about a week, the family receives visitors to help them mourn. In some orthodox families, if a child marries a non-Jew, the family will sit *shiva* for them, demonstrating that by marrying outside the faith, their child is dead to them. Families from all faiths and cultures disown their children for all kinds of reasons: for coming out if they are queer, marrying someone from another race or ethnic group, getting pregnant out of wedlock, or not following some sort of family or cultural norm.

While my parents were not religious at all, it nonetheless felt as if they had sat *shiva* for me. I don't get the sense that they made a conscious choice to consider me dead. Maybe keeping me emotionally alive meant they'd have to stay in touch with feelings they were unable to manage. Did they suppress painful or uncomfortable feelings to the point that they were no longer able to see me? Did they disassociate from me the way I disassociated from my memories? Whether or not they'd sat *shiva*, the impact on me was the same. I felt unaccepted and unseen all over again each time my parents took no action to attempt to engage with me.

***

My daughter Maya was born in the summer of 1996. I sent my parents a birth announcement despite our estrangement. One day, when Maya was a few weeks old, I came home from a walk with her. I entered the vestibule pushing a large carriage. My father and my nephew, who was about five years old, were leaving the building. They walked past us and my father showed no sign that he recognized me. I was livid. I understood if my father had no desire to talk to me, but how could he walk right by his own granddaughter whom he'd never seen? Adrenaline surged through me and I lost control.

I walked back outside. My father and nephew were halfway down the block. I screamed after my father, "So, you don't even want to see your granddaughter?"

He turned around, appearing dazed, frozen in place as if he had no idea who I was and what I might want. I yelled again, "I'm your daughter! Don't you want to see your granddaughter?"

He walked back slowly and sheepishly, holding my nephew's hand. He leaned over the carriage without saying a word to me. I turned to my nephew, "Do you want to see your cousin?" Looking confused, my nephew peeked into the carriage. Then my father took his hand and they both turned and walked off.

A Meeting is Brokered

From the moment Maya was born, Ann and her husband Reno doted on her. They had two sons, no daughters and no grandchildren at the time. They treated me like the daughter they never had and Maya like their own grandchild. For the first year or so of my daughter's life, Ann was "Gran." Having her in our lives was a true blessing.

As far as Ann was concerned, the sun rose when Maya came into the room. Ann sat on the floor and drummed on chairs with her, sang with her and overall simply adored her. In Ann's eyes, my daughter was the most beautiful, unique, intelligent, special child in the entire world. Loving Maya unconditionally, Ann played the role of grandmother perfectly. And she was there for me when I was ready to go back to work after my maternity leave.

"Ann, none of my clothes fit me anymore. I don't know what I'm gonna to wear."

"Let's go shopping. I can hold Maya while you try on clothes."

And she was there when Jeffrey and I needed a night out.

Mystery of Memory

"I'll watch the kids. You two go have a good time."

***

Ann did her best to get me to reconcile with my parents, though I resisted for a long time. After Maya was born, my parents sent me a check to start a college fund for her. They also sent a package that contained an antique-looking, white-but-yellowing infant gown that I must've worn soon after I was born and a black velvet dress with a lace collar. Of course I had no memory of the gown. I did remember the dress; it was one of my "dressy" dresses that I wore with black patent-leather shoes with straps for special occasions. The idea that my parents had treasured these items over the years melted some of the hardness in my heart.

At Ann's urging, in the winter of 1996, I allowed her to broker a meeting with my parents at her house for Chanukah so they could meet Maya, who was four months old. Jeffrey and I arrived with Maya and had brunch with my parents, Ann, and Reno. The meeting was cordial and, of course, they both had a chance to hold their granddaughter. While they were delighted to see her, compared to Ann neither of them was effusive or demonstrative. My mother held the baby, but without the usual "oohs and ahs," and proclamations of beauty that usually accompany holding a grandchild for the first time.

I realize now that I have always judged my mother through my narrow perspective of what constitutes an expression of love. I know my mother loved me and I know she was delighted to see her granddaughter. She simply didn't show her emotions—it wasn't who she was. I judged her harshly for that. After that brunch, my mother regularly came to my home to spend time with Maya and me. My father didn't.

IV. I Rest My Case

MOTHER'S DAY

I kept diaries for years but just before I moved to Japan from Alaska, I burned them all. I was going to store my belongings in my parents' attic and didn't want to risk their finding them. In the early 2000s, I threw away some other diaries because reading them was too painful. That left me with little to help in the process of writing this book. When I looked back over the last three decades, I knew I experienced periods of depression and intense pain. When I tried to bring specific incidents to mind, however, I drew a blank. I did find some diaries that I had written on my computer and not deleted. In reviewing them, I was surprised at how many painful memories I had completely put out of my mind. It's as if instead of storing these experiences in my accessible memory, they, along with the feelings accompanying them, got stored in the deep recesses of my unconscious.

While I didn't remember them, Jeffrey and I had problems in our marriage almost from the start. Whenever things went well, I'd forget the times when they were not. It was only through reviewing some diaries that I was able to recollect them.

The night before my first Mother's Day in 1997, I was exhausted from nursing Maya, helping Omar with his homework and a long week at work. What I wanted more than anything was to lie in bed with Jeffrey and just cuddle; I needed rest and attention. Instead, Jeffrey was cold and wouldn't even turn the TV off when I came into the bedroom. I went to bed angry and hurt and woke up on Mother's Day feeling the same. Jeffrey woke up, mumbled, "Happy Mother's Day," and went back to sleep. When Jeffrey got out of bed, I left Maya with him and went for a walk. I started to feel rage at my father.

I found myself in the phone booth around the corner from my house dialing my parents' number. I couldn't keep myself from banging my head against what had been a closed door for so long. I kept thinking that the reason they failed to respond to me the way I wanted them to must be because I hadn't communicated with them clearly or articulately enough. What if I reached out by phone instead of in writing and tried to have a heart-to-heart talk?

My father answered the phone. In a gentle, soft voice, I said, "Hi Da, I think we need to talk."

"About what?" he said, his voice tight and angry.

The rage bubbled back up, "About the fact that you molested me!"

"Your therapist fucked you up. I never did anything to you!"

He'd never mentioned my therapist before. His response felt as if he spat in my face. Crying, I went home, got into bed and sobbed.

My Supreme Court Brief

A week or so after the phone call with my father, my mother called. Trying to assuage my anger at my father, she said, "Let's just forget about the whole thing."

"What whole thing? How can I forget about something that we haven't even dealt with?"

A few days after this call, I sent my parents a ten-page letter. I saw it as a last-ditch, final effort to get them to admit that my father had molested me, my final appeal to them to validate my reality and enable me to close the case. While I didn't want to admit it, I also hoped to overcome my own self-doubt.

The letter, which I called my "Supreme Court Brief," was written like a legal document. I had no witnesses or corroboration so I had to make my arguments based solely on circumstantial evidence.

I used the standard law-school example of someone walking to a cabin in the woods shortly after a snowfall and finding one person alive and another person murdered. While the person alive in the cabin could have been the killer, a set of footprints in the snow outside leading to and from the cabin constitutes circumstantial evidence that a second person had been in the cabin and committed the crime. If the person inside the cabin had committed the crime, who made the footprints that led away from the cabin?

In my letter, I enumerated what I saw as the circumstantial evidence—the footprints— in my case. These included: the bizarrely calm way that both my parents reacted when Pierre confronted them; that I was depressed when I was six years old; the relief and release I felt after experiencing my vision; and my father having told me that while he couldn't remember it, "something must have happened."

My parents' response was a terse letter saying they couldn't acknowledge what didn't happen. I was baffled and hurt to the quick. I felt that I had poured my heart out to my parents. How could they have nothing to say to me? I felt depleted. I had no more to give.

***

When my daughter's first birthday came around, I didn't invite my parents to her party. Ann bought my daughter a special dress and served in the role of grandparent. My parents sent a gift: a set of large Lego blocks. I didn't even acknowledge it. I can see now how painful that must have been for them. They were trying to reach out to me, but I didn't see it that way.

I couldn't understand what I saw as their failure to try to connect with me. I wondered why they couldn't even simply validate my pain by writing, "I'm sorry you're in so much pain, how can we help?" I showed a copy of the "Brief" to a friend of mine a year or so later to give him a sense of how I had reached out to my parents and how they had not responded to my overtures. I was shocked when he said, "Deb, you're kind of intimidating."

I was so engulfed in my own hurt and pain that I couldn't even imagine what they might be going through. I couldn't see my own power. It wasn't until years later that I saw how my words came across. I was convinced I was being vulnerable and open; I didn't realize how angry and combative my tone was. How could they be vulnerable in response to that?

My Marriage

In early 1998, I entered the American University/NTL Master's program in organization development. I traveled to Washington, DC once a month for three days of classes. During those times, I allowed Jeffrey to take Maya to see my parents at their home. While I had no interest in seeing them, I didn't want to deprive my daughter of having some connection to her roots—but I wouldn't let them see her unless Jeffrey was there to supervise.

***

Issues related to my being molested made me a difficult partner. At times, Jeffrey was understanding. If I felt anxious and tense, I'd ask him to lay down with me and put his hand on my chest over my heart, to help me feel secure. He did. On some occasions, I felt reassured. On others, words flew into my mind that I felt like screaming out loud: "Leave me alone! Stop it! Go away!" and/or "Help me!"

Sex could be enjoyable or it could feel horrendous. Sometimes I wanted to tell him to stop. Yet, I didn't feel that I could.

I hadn't experienced sexual problems with men in my life before being with Jeffrey, or with Jeffrey before we were married. But this was the first time I had lived with a man. Living with and being in a long-term committed relationship made me feel trapped. I felt obligated to meet his physical needs.

I reached out once to a friend, and told her how hard it was to be intimate with Jeffrey sometimes, because of being molested. She made clear that meeting my husband's physical needs had to take precedence over my emotional needs.

Whenever I didn't feel emotionally connected with Jeffrey, I didn't want to be touched sexually at all. I wrestled with societal expectations to "please your man" versus meeting my own needs. There were times when Jeffrey came home after work, angry about something, but told me there was nothing wrong. Then, after not talking to me the entire evening, he would come to bed and want to have sex; I repeatedly told him that I needed to feel emotionally connected before I could be physically intimate. When he continued to approach me in ways I asked him not to, I felt violated.

When I was unresponsive, Jeffrey sometimes accused me of being frigid or asked me how he was supposed to meet his needs. I began to think I was defective. I hated myself for being damaged.

***

I was an unpredictable parent with loose boundaries. I'd experienced my parents as emotionally unavailable—I wanted my children to experience warmth and feelings of safety. I became a fierce protective lioness. Often I went too far. I was incapable of allowing Maya to experience pain if I could do anything about it. If she carelessly lost something, I'd replace it. If Omar broke a rule and I told him he couldn't watch TV, I'd relent when he came to me with an affectionate apology. I wanted Maya to feel heard, and allowed her to express her feelings any way she wanted. She had trouble, as a result, understanding the difference between experiencing her feelings and acting them out.

My sensitivity to betrayal had an impact as well. Once, when Omar was a teenager, he stole some money from me; something many teenagers do. I punished him completely out of proportion; I took away all his video games, his CDs and CD player, his Xbox player, and almost everything else in his room. Then, having never laid hands on him before, I slapped his face in anger.

I held myself to an unreasonably high standard but didn't hold Jeffrey to it; I simply took over. Omar was supposed to visit his mother, Louise, on alternate weekends, but she often failed to show up. Jeffrey railed at Louise, sometimes in front of Omar, or blamed

Omar for things out of his control, such as Louise forgetting to pick up Omar or not returning all his clothes. I didn't want Omar to hear Jeffrey badmouthing Louise so I took over as liaison, calling her every other Thursday to remind her to pick up her son.

I felt Jeffrey didn't appreciate what it took to be the one who communicated and maintained a good relationship with Louise. It's quite possible Jeffrey would have been able to reach détente with Louis on his own, but I never allowed myself to find out.

Some of our issues were the result of cultural expectations. I had a professional degree and was working as a law school administrator. He had not completed college and worked as a tradesperson. I had a steady income while, as a small business owner, he did not. I had no problem with being the major breadwinner in the family. Jeffrey, however, felt the weight of society's expectation that, as a man, he be the one to financially support the family. For him, providing supporting meant bringing in income. For me, it meant spending time together. What I wanted more than anything was for him to spend time on the weekends with the children, especially Omar. I wanted Omar to have quality time with his father, particularly as he became a teenager. Jeffrey got angry when I pressured him to spend less time at work.

We argued over money. He made promises about what he could contribute, but wasn't always able to follow through. I wasn't disturbed that he wasn't providing enough income. I was upset because I didn't think he was being realistic or transparent with me.

I also felt the weight of gender expectations: cleaning the house, taking care of the children, changing diapers, ensuring homework got done, going to PTA meetings, making doctor's appointments, doing the laundry, etc. I resented Jeffrey's not helping with household tasks and not recognizing my contributions. If I ever complained, he responded as if his work was more exhausting than mine.

When things went well, I would be in an almost frenetic high. But when Jeffrey was angry, I walked on eggshells. I wasn't afraid of him hitting me; I was afraid of his anger, his yelling and what he would say. Constantly worried about upsetting him, I felt myself becoming smaller, my life constricting. Despite my logical mind knowing Jeffrey would never physically hurt me, my body was in constant fight-flight-freeze mode. Frightened as I felt in the marriage, my greater fear was not having a man in my life to love and protect me, because that would prove how worthless I was. I couldn't be in a healthy loving marriage until I loved myself.

Reconciliation and Acceptance

Sometime in the winter of 2000, my anger dissipated and I began spending time with my parents again. Maybe it was because my parents created a college account for Omar. I felt that indicated their understanding of how important he was in my life. This was the first time they had in any way treated him as their grandchild. In any event, my anger was spent and I had come to a place of acceptance.

Years before, when my parents failed to verify my memories, I concluded that they didn't love me, and that I was not worth being loved. If I were worthy of being loved, I reasoned, they would've done anything in their power to keep from losing me—even if it meant exploring deeply within themselves to see if there were things they were repressing. I yearned for my parents to validate my experience. I needed them to say they believed me so I could feel worthy of love and love myself, but they didn't. I had to let go of my need for them to provide me with confirmation. The only way I could do that was to be able see myself as worthy of love.

Gradually, I accepted that no matter what I did, my parents were not going to respond to me the way I yearned and hoped for. They were not going to acknowledge my reality. Through this process of acceptance, I let go of my judgment, anger, and expectations and finally stopped trying to make them validate me.

Maintaining my anger and resentment was toxic and served no purpose. I could not be at peace until I forgave my parents. Many people see forgiveness as if it means condoning another's action. That is not the way I see it. My forgiveness was not a gift to my parents. It was a gift to myself for my own well-being. If I didn't forgive them, I would remain a prisoner of my own anger and so I did.

In December of 2000, I invited my parents and my brother's family to celebrate Chanukah at my home. Even though I had been in touch with my parents on and off for years, I hadn't been in contact with Aaron since I cut off communication with my parents in 1994. It was the first time Aaron and his wife Sarah met Maya, who was about four years old, and the first time I met my niece, Caroline, who is about a year older than Maya. The two of them connected right away. We began to get together for family dinners, but we never discussed our years of estrangement. We moved on as if nothing had happened.

For a while, spending time with my parents continued to feel uncomfortable. At first I was doing it for the sake of my daughter. Then, after a few years, I was able to spend time with them on my own, feeling comfortable and safe.

I came to be grateful for the relationship they had with Maya. I loved to see my father play checkers with her or to watch her help my mother set the table.

Around this time, I graduated from my masters program, left the law school and became Director of the Law School Consortium Project, which focused on supporting law schools and solo practitioners to meet the legal needs of low and moderate-income communities.

Jeffrey and I divorced in 2001. Omar continued to live with me so the children could be together and have some stability. In 2003, I established my own firm, working as a consultant and coach helping leaders and their teams transform themselves and the world by tapping into their wisdom and creative potential.

***

Since we had first reconciled, I never raised the topic of my memories with my parents again. On one occasion in June of 2005, however, apropos to nothing, my father did. My daughter and I had gone to my parents' house for dinner and a family friend was there as well. We'd finished dinner and I was in the kitchen with my father rinsing the dishes so he could load them into the dishwasher. My mother, our friend, and my daughter were in hearing distance in the dining room, separated from the kitchen only by a large island.

As we stood working together, he said, "I've seen lots of therapists. I saw one before Aaron was born and then after Aaron was suicidal..." He listed a few more until he ended with, "and another one when you were giving me a hard time."

I was shocked. I didn't say anything. I was going to just let it go because there didn't seem to be any use in responding in any way.

"You don't still believe that, do you? That I molested you?" His tone had an edge; it felt similar to the way he made biting comments to me as a child that left me feeling powerless and humiliated. This time it didn't have the same effect.

Calmly, I replied, "Yes, I do."

Without looking at me, and continuing to load the dishwasher, he muttered something about how my therapist had damaged me, or something like that.

Still in shock, I said, "If you really want to have this conversation, I don't think this is the time or the place."

He nodded. Then, still not looking at me, in a harsh tone, he said, "I know what he did – that therapist of yours did something when he came here."

I simply said, "I don't agree with you so we'll just have to agree to disagree." After finishing with the dishes, I went back to the dining room table. I could feel my heart beating rapidly in my throat and my nerves and every fiber of my body felt tense and wound up. I hadn't felt that way in years.

Neither of us spoke of the incident after that.

***

Shortly before his eighty-fifth birthday in January of 2006, my mother called. She wanted me to write about my father for his birthday because he told her that people always say nice things after people die when it's too late for them to hear it. She told me she wanted me to write it because, "Daddy says you're the most articulate one in the family."

Writing about my father was a challenge, I didn't know much about him as a person. I decided to compare his childhood, growing up with almost nothing, with what he had been able to provide for his children. I read it to him at the family dinner for his birthday

For Da – January 26, 2006

Daddy is a man who grew up with very little, but made sure his children grew up differently.

When he was a child, he spent his free time helping prepare and apply labels to the cans of cleaning fluid his father tried to sell to support the family. His children spent their free time doing things like going to summer camp and skiing.

Daddy put himself through City College while his children both attended expensive private colleges out of state (not to mention a private high school), having to work only for spending money, not tuition, room, or board.

He came from a childhood with limited experiences. It did not, however, leave him with a closed mind. He and Mom traveled to more countries than most people even know exist. And, wherever they went he would gamely try whatever food was available. In fact, one of the rules of our family was that we had to take at least one bite of any food before we could decide if we liked it or not. Being willing to take on new experiences and try new things is a habit he passed down to us.

Now, we all know that sometimes, he would not be anxious to embark on a trip. He took some trips only because he knew Mom would leave him behind if he refused to go, but once he got to wherever they were going, he would throw himself wholeheartedly into the experience. Sometimes he would go a bit too far. When he and Mom visited me in Japan, he insisted on learning to ask some questions in Japanese—like, "Where is the train station?" What he neglected to consider, however, was that no matter how well he might ask the question, he would have no way of understanding the answer.

Daddy is a man who grew up with very little. He made sure his children and his grandchildren would grow up differently. Now, Daddy is rich in ways that money cannot buy. He is rich with the love of his wife, his children, and his grandchildren. We love you very much. Happy Birthday!!!

I SHARE A PIECE OF MY STORY

I felt compelled to write about my being molested for years. But while my parents were alive, I couldn't bring myself to do anything that would publicly expose or humiliate them. The closest I came to writing about it was in 2006, when I wrote the book *Repairing the Quilt of Humanity: A Metaphor for Healing and Reparation.* The focus of the book was not incest; it was racism and other forms of oppression. I used the three layers of a quilt as a metaphor to explore the impact of various isms at the three levels of individual, group and system. I tried to use the lens of my experience of childhood sexual abuse, which I defined as psychological oppression, as a way to help others gain insight into the psychological trauma caused by racism and other forms of oppression. Just as the pain and suffering resulting from being sexually molested is invisible to others, the psychological damage caused by racism is invisible to individuals who have not experienced or learned about it. I wanted to make these injuries visible.

I was candid about having been molested and shared some of how it impacted my life. But I shared no specific details about the experience or the identity of the person who victimized me. I identified the perpetrator simply as a family member, but provided no further information. I did everything I could to protect my parents. I even dedicated the book to them.

To my parents: "The fruit doesn't fall far from the tree." I am proud to have fallen from your branches. Thank you for fertilizing me with the values I cherish most in the world, including the importance of standing up for what is right, for modeling a life of working to repair the world, and for loving me through challenging times. May your tree continue to thrive in the garden of the world. I am proud to be your daughter and I love you deeply.

I meant what I wrote. I value the legacy of social and racial justice my parents left me.

Writing *Repairing the Quilt of Humanity* was healing. It was cathartic and cleansing to own my story without the need for my parents to verify it. I felt like a different person after I published it. I had let go and taken the final step in the journey from spending years feeling like a victim, and have that as my life narrative, to being a survivor. My memory of sexual abuse was no longer the definition of who I was, but an experience that I'd gone through. I felt whole. My childhood no longer loomed large in my thoughts.

***

I had great angst about whether or not to give my parents copies of the book even though I knew I couldn't keep it a secret. My father, who loved to surf the Internet, could stumble across it.

I reached out to my Aunt Beryl before I made my decision. Beryl was not actually my aunt, but I considered her family. She was my aunt Joan's closest friend and I guessed Joan had spoken with her about the molestation but I wasn't sure. Beryl took care of Joan until she died in November of 2000 after suffering from Alzheimer's. The true nature of Joan and Beryl's relationship was another family secret that was simply not "seen."

My mother's family had known Beryl since she was a child. She went to high school with my mother and aunt. At some point in the early 1970s, Joan and Beryl traveled together all over the world. Soon, Beryl was coming to family events such as Passover and Thanksgiving. They each had their own place, but Joan spent every weekend at Beryl's one-bedroom apartment on the Upper West Side, that had only one double bed. On New Year's Day, they always hosted a special brunch for family and friends at Beryl's apartment. No one ever discussed the possibility that they might be lovers.

I went to visit Beryl shortly after I had given her the book. "Did you have a chance to read it?"

"Yes."

"What did you think?"

"I think it's well-written and the analysis was well done."

She didn't say that she was proud, but I felt it from her and it brought me to tears. That was what I longed to hear from my parents.

"Do you think I should give my parents a copy of it?"

"Well, I'm of two minds, though you did give them tribute in it."

Then I asked her, "Did Joan ever talk to you about my being molested?"

"Yes, she did. She always believed you and she never changed her mind."

While it was heartening to hear that someone in the family believed me, it was painful that I didn't have that same understanding from my parents or brother.

***

I remained torn about sharing the *Repairing the Quilt of Humanity* with my parents. On the one hand, it could open a can of worms, and on the other hand, maybe it could be a vehicle for finally getting things out in the open.

I had recently finished a course in hypnosis and Neuro-Linguistic Programming for use in my coaching practice. I trained under a certified instructor named Frank. I met him when conducting some training. He was the internal human resources contact at the client organization and we co-facilitated the work. He had a small coaching practice on the side. Once I finished the course, Frank and I agreed to coach each other on alternate weeks. I decided I would use one of my sessions to help me decide whether or not to give the book to my parents.

Frank put me into a trance. My throat became tight. I experienced the sense of screaming internally to myself about how scared I was, but I realized that I was no longer a helpless child and had a strong sense of my own voice. I no longer wanted to stay silenced out of fear. While in the trance, I asked myself whether or not I should give my parents the book. I sensed the presence of my younger self who answered, "Not if you're going to keep denying me!"

This experience helped me realize that my fear was not so much that my parents or brother wouldn't verify my truth, but that I would once again doubt myself if they didn't.

When I got in touch with my own inner voice, I felt clear and centered. I believed in myself. I decided to give them my book not to get validation, but to honor my truth and myself. Sharing my story with them was my way of acknowledging myself. I wanted them to know who I had become and what was important to me. I also wanted them to know they had given me a lot for which I was grateful and that I loved them.

I hoped that in reading the dedication they would understand that *Repairing the Quilt of Humanity* was in no way meant as an attack, but rather an attempt to share my journey with them. The book contained a section on the importance of acknowledgment as part of the healing process. I hoped that when they read it, my parents might see my pain instead of my anger; that reading that section might break down whatever defense mechanisms my father had in place to keep his memories repressed and bring about some change in response to my pleading for his acknowledgement. In writing my "Supreme Court Brief," I tried to make my case to my parents through logic and rational thinking. Perhaps, I thought, *Repairing the Quilt of Humanity* would touch and open up their hearts.

I gave my parents and my brother gift-wrapped copies on the same day. I started with my mother. I called her and told her I wanted to meet someplace where we could be alone. She was having breakfast with a friend at a diner in her neighborhood and I met her afterwards. It was a warm day and we walked to a nearby church. It was a lovely, peaceful place. We sat on a wooden bench near the church garden, under a small tree.

Before giving her the book, I told her, "I'm giving this to you. It's a book I wrote that I hope will help you better understand me and strengthen our relationship. It's mainly about racism, but from the perspective of my childhood experience."

She looked straight into my eyes and nodded. I interpreted that as an indication that she understood I was talking about the molestation. She took the book out of the small gift bag and unwrapped the tissue paper. I asked her to read the dedication, so she'd see that it was written with love, not anger. We sat in silence for a while and then I said, "Mom, if you want to discuss the book we can, but I need to be clear that my experience is my truth and it isn't debatable or negotiable. And, it's not like you have to speak now or forever hold your peace, but I need to tell you that, even if you didn't believe me, I can't understand why you didn't reach out to me knowing how much pain I was in." She nodded, reached out and gave me a hug. We sat in silence for a while longer.

Then, I said, "I want to give a copy to Daddy as well."

"Do you want me to give it to him?" she asked.

"No, I'll give it to him later when I walk you back home. Are you hungry Ma?"

"No, just thirsty."

"OK, let's go."

I walked back home with her to give my father his copy. My mother had been suffering from arthritis and stenosis and had difficulty with stairs. We climbed up the steps of the stoop slowly. I followed her pace to stay alongside her. We walked into the building's vestibule, down the hall to the foot of the stairs. There were two long flights of stairs to reach my parents' apartment. Because of my mother's arthritis, they had a chairlift on the stairway.

"Go ahead, don't wait for me," she said as she sat on the lift.

I was relieved to be able to go ahead of her. I wanted to be alone with my father when I gave him the book.

I found him sitting at the dining room table reading the newspaper. I sat down next to him, my back to the kitchen.

"I have something important I want to talk to you about." I saw his body tense, he sat up straighter in the chair and his eyes narrowed. My heart was beating fast and my words came quickly. I rushed because I knew my mother would walk in at any moment. I hadn't planned this well, but pushed forward. I felt compelled to allay his anxiety immediately and this served to make my words come out even faster.

The way I spoke with my father was not the same slow, thoughtful manner I had used with my mother. When she unwrapped and opened the book, it was clear that she understood my intent that it was a gift. My father, on the other hand, didn't appear to view it that way.

"Da, I want to give you something and I want you to know that I'm giving it to you because I love you. I wrote a book about racism that also discusses my experiences as a child."

"So, it's about me," he retorted.

"No, the book is not about you. It doesn't even mention you. It's really about racism."

I had him read the dedication. Then he looked up and asked, "What do you want me to do with this?" He was curt. He didn't ask me any other questions. That was it.

I remained calm. "Well, I'd like you to read it. I think it's a well-written book and deals with the issue of racism and I think it'll help you understand me."

As my mother came in, he jumped up from the table and muttered that he needed to write me a check. Seeing that I had given the book to my father, my mother whispered to me, "I'll tell you what happens."

My father strode back into the room with a check. I had asked him for a loan a week before, but hadn't expected him to write me a check that day. I looked at it and realized that he had forgotten to sign it.

***

I called my brother at work and arranged to bring the book to his office. He came down to the lobby when I arrived. "I can't talk long. I'm crazy busy upstairs."

"I don't need much time. I have something to give you. It was hard to decide whether or not to give it to you, but I decided to because I love you and I want you to better understand me." I had tears in my eyes. He nodded and took the book.

***

I didn't hear from my parents or my brother. The only reason I could think of for them not having called is that they hadn't yet had time to read it, but even that left me angry because it's a short book.

Finally, I called my parents. My father answered, "Hey Da, I tried calling earlier. Where were you guys?"

"We were at a funeral," he told me.

"Sorry to hear that. Whose was it?"

He mentioned someone I didn't know. "That name's not familiar. Who is that?"

"I don't feel like talking to you right now," he said abruptly and hung up the phone.

My chest became tense and my throat tightened. The familiar sensation of being all alone, unprotected and crazy came over me. To help me get through these feelings, I called my friend Lewis. Through tears, I said, "Lewis, my father just hung up on me and no one in my family has called since I gave them the book. Am I the one who's crazy?"

"No, you're not crazy. When I was a kid, my grandmother beat me almost every day. Some days, she locked me in the closet. I knew what she was doing was wrong. And that's what helped me survive. With you, the abuse felt wrong, but at the same time, you felt responsible for what happened so you don't have that same sense of clarity. So when you vacillate between feeling afraid of being called crazy or blamed for what happened, you victimize yourself all over again."

Hearing Lewis' voice and knowing that he loved, supported and believed me, enabled me to move through the fear. I decided that if they didn't want to talk to me, it was their loss and I didn't reach out to any of them.

After about a week my mother called. "I haven't heard from you in a while. Why haven't you called?"

"Well, when I called the last time, Daddy said he didn't want to talk to me," I answered.

"Well, that's him, not me."

Differentiating herself from my father when it came to me was unlike my mother. In spite of being shored up by my talk with Lewis, I was afraid to ask her anything.

When I next called, my father spoke to me as if nothing had happened. Neither of my parents ever brought up the book again, nor did my brother and neither did I.

About a year or two after giving the book to Aaron, I decided to ask him about it. "You've never said anything to me about what you thought about my book?"

I can't remember which it was, but he either said, "Well, I just preferred to keep my head in the sand" or "If you don't have anything nice to say…." I didn't ask him anything else.

I Find Peace

I realized that it was ten years almost to the day that I had given birth to my daughter. Giving my family a copy of my book was like another form of birth, in this case to a new life in relation to my family.

Interacting with my parents became different. I was not only able to feel comfortable with them, I came to enjoy time with them, usually over a meal, and it felt natural. I came to accept our mutual love. Particularly in the last years of their lives, I became the person they relied on most to drive them places, pick up groceries, take them to doctor's appointments, provide computer technology assistance or even serve as a relationship mediator when the two of them locked horns.

One Passover, my mother and I were in her kitchen preparing dinner. "Here Deb, put on an apron so you don't ruin your clothes. So, which recipe should we use for the *haroses*?" (*Haroses* is made with apples and nuts to represent the mortar the Jewish slaves used to work with when they were enslaved in Egypt.)

"Let's use this one." I said pointing to the one my grandmother always used to use.

"OK, I'll start cooking the eggs for the egg noodles while you make the *haroses*," said my mother.

"Alright, I'll cut the eggs once they're ready." My grandmother used to be the one to make the egg noodles for the chicken soup. Now, my mother and I were doing it. This required making thin crepe-like pancakes with the eggs. Once they cooled, I rolled them up and sliced them, making paper-thin noodles.

I loved it when we were in the kitchen together. We had never done that when I was a child. Now, we were simply present with each other as we worked in silence. It was special knowing that we were using my grandmother's recipes for the *haroses* and the homemade egg noodles, and that we were doing what the women in my family have done together for years. While my mother cooked the eggs, I chopped up the apples and walnuts. Standing in the kitchen with my mother on those occasions, I was relaxed and calm and took pleasure from our time together.

Other times, my father and I sat together at the dining room table. He'd say something like, "Deb, I'm reading this wonderful book, *Constantine's Sword*. It's fascinating," or "Deb, did you see the Op-Ed piece in the *Times* this morning?"

On one occasion, after we'd been reconciled for about five years, I sat with my father as we usually did, waiting for dinner to be ready, when out of the blue he asked, "Deb, why do you feel so distant? I don't feel that you're connected to me."

I was surprised by his question, but responded, "I'm not sure why you feel I'm not connected. Maybe it's because there are things I've experienced that you haven't accepted or acknowledged, so I can't bring all of myself to our relationship because it doesn't feel safe. If you're asking me if I love you, I do. I come here and spend time with the two of you because I enjoy being in your presence. Being close and sharing space with you and Mom means a lot to me. That's my way of showing my love. If I'm in the kitchen with Mom helping her with dinner, that time is precious to me. Sitting at the table and talking to you is precious, too. If you can't feel the love that I bring, I have no idea how else I could show it to you."

After that conversation, my relationship with my father changed significantly. He began to depend on me in certain ways. Once, he asked me to review a letter to the editor he wanted to submit to the *New York Times* about getting old and I gave him some feedback on it. Afterwards, he called to let me know that the letter had been published and that a stranger called to let him know how much he appreciated it, which meant a lot to him. I was whole-heartedly happy for him and congratulated him.

My father came to see me almost as his counselor and talked to me about things he was worried about. By then, my parents were both in their late 80s.

Once, I was visiting my parents and my father drew me aside. "Your mother wants to go on cruise with her friend Thelma. It's a ridiculous idea. What if she falls? She could get hurt. Will you talk some sense into her?"

"Da, Mom could fall and get hurt at home without going anyplace. This is something she wants to do. You can't just keep her cooped up in the apartment when she wants to continue living her life actively."

Grudgingly, he stopped fighting her on it.

He kept lists of everything, on the backs of used envelopes and scratch paper. One Sunday after brunch, he showed me a piece of paper. "Look, here are all your mother's prescriptions. She's driving me crazy because she keeps forgetting to renew them and she gets mad at me if I talk to her about it. What am I supposed to do?"

"You're driving yourself crazy because you keep obsessing and worrying about it. If she doesn't want your help and she doesn't remember to renew her prescriptions, she'll just have to deal with running out of them."

With a deep sigh he said, "OK."

Once he said, "I really enjoy these talks," and I did, too. Being in connection with my parents while letting go of expecting anything from them was healing.

V. Self-Doubt and Discovery

My Parents Pass Away

My parents passed away six weeks apart from each other in 2012 and 2013. For almost a decade, I had a warm, loving relationship with them. I feel blessed that we had these times together.

In the last few years of my father's life, he was miserable. He was diagnosed with cancer and told me he experienced no joy in life. He was too weak to go out, his appetite disappeared, and he was depressed. His unhappiness got to the point that he asked me to get information for him about the Hemlock Society, a right-to-die organization. Sometimes, I sat quietly with him and held his hand. On one such occasion, he told me, "You're a great comfort to me." That meant a lot to me. I was finally able to accept that the love he gave me was real.

The night before my father died, I was spoon-feeding him some ice cream when he got agitated.

"Where's my wallet?" he asked.

I handed it to him. "It's OK, Da. You've taken care of everything. Mom's going to be fine."

He passed away early the next morning.

A few weeks after my father died, my mother fell—most likely breaking a hip. She refused to go to the hospital. Despite being bed-ridden, she was completely lucid until the last few days of her life. The day before she passed, she was semi-unconscious. I was with her the entire day and spent the night at her bedside because I sensed it was her last. I lay down on my parents' bed, next to her hospital bed, and held her hand. Around midnight, I couldn't keep my eyes open, so I set my alarm to wake me every ten minutes. I woke from one of my naps, and instead of hearing her slow, labored breathing, there was silence. She was gone.

Being with my parents on the last days of their lives, I knew they could feel my love as I felt theirs.

I Decide to Confront My Self-Doubt Head On

Before my parents died, I had come to accept they loved me. However, believing that my parents loved me made it difficult to believe that my father had molested me. The voice of doubt in my head returned and became loud. "Daddy loved me so he couldn't possibly have molested me." I decided to confront my self-doubt by writing this book and engaging in an exploration for myself.

When I started the writing process, I was at my desk writing, first thing in the morning. Expressing myself left me euphoric and empowered. But one morning the bottom fell out. I had no desire to work, write, go to a yoga class, talk on the phone to anyone, nothing. I slipped into the familiar pit of depression with the loud shame-inducing voice saying, "Who the hell do you think you are to write this book? What if nothing really happened to you? You're a fraud and there is nothing you can do to bring meaning into your life. You're worthless."

Reaching out for help when I feel this worthless and vulnerable is a challenge. I'm afraid that if I reach out and don't get support, it'll prove how worthless I really am. In the past, I wallowed, holing up until the depression eventually passed. This experience was different—I was afraid of how powerful my desire to die was.

I reached out to Yvette, a dear friend. With my words distorted by tears, I said, "I just feel like dying. I'm so worthless. My parents loved me so nothing could have happened. I must be crazy. I must have made it all up."

Yvette was quick to offer me consolation and reassurance. "No Deb. You're not crazy. Not having memories and feeling crazy is one of the things that most incest survivors experience."

"Really?" I stammered.

"Yes, I've done a lot of writing groups with women and this is common. You are not crazy and I love you."

For years, I had believed I was the only person who had memory fragments without context or being able to surface more. My inability to come up with "data" evoked not only self-doubt, but self-hatred. I thought I was unique in not being able to recover more memories and feeling crazy as a result. Yvette's words gave me strength.

***

After talking with Yvette, my feelings of worthlessness dissipated. I had never before put my two memories into writing. As I wrote, the somatic memories, and the physical sensations associated with them, started to surface. I realized that my body had a story to tell me, if I allowed it. I stopped trying to force visual or auditory memories to come to mind. I simply allowed myself to be present in my body, without struggling to attach words or meaning to what I was experiencing. I could feel the emotions—loneliness, a desire to be held, the shock and sense of something being wrong, fear, powerlessness, shame and guilt. My rational mind could use defense mechanisms to repress my memories, but the emotions and feelings of the experiences remained in my body.

While my defense mechanisms couldn't make these somatic memories disappear, they were nonetheless busy at work. Some days I felt focused and energetic. Other days, even though I wasn't depressed, I felt lethargic, drained and unable to get out of bed. I judged myself harshly on those days, calling myself lazy. I didn't' realize the emotional toll of writing this book. As I continued to write, I came to understand my lethargy was another defense mechanism. Toward the end of the final draft, I came down with a cold lasting an entire week—my body was protecting me from too much pain at once. When I was not aware of my own needs, my body came to the rescue. I came to see that these mechanisms had served to defend me my whole life.

One morning, after some fruitful writing, I took a break and went to a yoga class. The class was in a large room with windows along one wall that let natural light in. I arrived early, lay down on my mat, closed my eyes and waited for class to begin. Then, tears came to my eyes. I felt ashamed, dirty and tainted. I started to feel nauseas. My internal voice shouted, "GET OFF ME!!" and my heart started racing as I felt the physical sensation of wanting to push someone away

I had to make a strong effort to keep from crying throughout the class, but by the end my heartbeat had slowed to a normal pace. My memories hadn't disappeared into the ether; they existed in these physical sensations and the emotions they contained.

I Become a Detective

Until about a year after my parents died, I had never considered asking any of my parents' friends what, if anything, my parents told them about my memories. Once I started writing this book, I knew I had to reach out to some of them as part of my "investigation."

The first person I reached out to was Lily, the woman who recognized me in the funeral parlor when my mother didn't. She had been my mother's friend since they were both in kindergarten.

I sat at my desk in my home office with my legs crossed and tucked under me. The room was dark; the only light came from the screen of my laptop. I couldn't pick up the phone, I felt debilitated, with a weight sitting on my chest. Despite my decision to reach out to Lily, it felt like too much effort. I was afraid of what I might hear and how painful it might be. But I knew I needed to do this if I ever wanted to be at peace.

I made myself pick up the phone. After the briefest of greetings, I asked, "Lily, did you know that there were times that I wasn't in communication with my parents?"

"Yes, I remember that." Lily said

"Did my mother ever tell you why?" I asked.

Lily paused briefly. "Yes, you were having trouble with your father, but I can't remember more than that. Why are you asking?"

I told Lily about my vision and how my memories had come to me. As I told her how my parents responded when my therapist Pierre confronted them, I started to cry. "Lily, what kind of parent responds that way? Why didn't my mother call me to see how I was feeling? How could they be so calm?" I moved from my desk chair to lie on the floor on my back. "My father acknowledged that something happened and then, years later, he took it back."

By the time I told her that he had recanted, tears were pouring out of me. I was surprised. I thought all this pain was behind me. The area on the left side of my chest under my rib cage ached. It felt like my heart was broken.

"Do you remember at my grandfather's funeral how my mother didn't even recognize me? My father didn't recognize me either. How could my own parents not have recognized me? You recognized me immediately."

Lily listened and expressed no surprise or doubt while I spoke. She didn't question the veracity of what I told her. That alone felt good. The tears subsided and I became calm.

Despite my sobbing, and as if this surprised her, Lily calmly asked, "So, this is still bothering you?"

"It's not bothering me in the sense that I have anger or resentment toward my parents. I reconciled with them before they died. But it hurts that neither of them ever validated my memories."

With a deep sigh, Lily said, "Well, you just push it aside." I interpreted "it" to mean anything that is too painful to accept.

She went on to say, "You deny it because you don't want to acknowledge it. People often choose not to acknowledge something because to acknowledge it would mean that they would have to do something about it. They can't change what happened. It's past and over and they would rather not think about it. It's easier to just forget about the whole thing."

The tears came again in full force as I pleaded, "Lily, I just need someone to validate what happened."

"You validated it and your mother did. It seems to me that I knew about it and she said something. It's very vague to me now, but she did," Lily said.

Hearing Lily say that, I assumed she was saying that my mother had told her that she had believed me. At once, a sense of calm and lightness came over me. It was like being covered tenderly with a soft blanket. I had a sense of letting go—as if a deeper level of healing had occurred and a piece of me that had been out of alignment for a long time had finally slipped back into place. Those words from the woman who had been my mother's best friend since childhood, who knew both my parents well, was like salve on a deep wound; like water to a dried-out plant. I sensed parts of me that had been dry, tight and dormant, relax, unfurl and come back to life.

I tried to ask Lily for more details, but she said she couldn't remember. Then, I changed the subject and asked her, "Lily, did you know that I wrote a book?"

"No, I didn't. What was it about?" Lily asked.

"It was mainly about racism, but I used my experience of sexual abuse as a lens to view it. I was hurt and disappointed that neither of my parents ever said anything to me about it after I gave them the book. I thought they'd have been proud of me for writing about racial justice." The tears and pain came back as I said those words, but it was a tender pain. It was grief rather than anger.

"Well, I'd love to read your book," Lily said.

"OK, I'll send you a copy," I said.

I was delighted when Lily expressed interest in my book. She shared the same beliefs and values as my parents. I longed to hear from her about how I was carrying on my parent's social justice legacy. Praise from her would have felt tantamount to praise from my parents.

Mystery of Memory

***

Anxious to hear what Lily would say about my book, I called her a few weeks after I sent it to her.

"So, did you have a chance to read my book?" I asked nervously.

"I did," Lily replied.

"What'd you think?"

"It was very interesting," Lily said.

I was taken aback. This wasn't the response I had anticipated. I also sensed a difference in her tone from our last phone call. She was reserved and somewhat standoff-ish. I tried to stay calm and curious. "What do you mean by 'interesting'?" I asked.

"Well," she said, "I wondered why you didn't say more about your mother in the book."

I didn't understand Lily's question, and feeling frustrated I tried to remain curious. "The book wasn't about my parents. Why would I have written about her?" I asked.

Lily gave me a vague answer. When I asked her to tell me more about what she thought, in an abrupt tone, she stated, "I don't know what else to say."

Her response was totally unexpected. I was confused, disappointed and hurt. Not only had she not said anything about the content of the book, but she wasn't willing to talk about it any further. I felt paralyzed by her response and the mixture of emotions I was experiencing, so I had no idea what else I could say. We said our goodbyes after making plans for me to visit her in St. Petersburg, where her oldest daughter, Kay, lived as well.

After getting off the phone I thought about what Lily had said. I didn't know how to interpret her words. I was stumped. What else could I have said? I wished I'd said, "Hmm, people usually use the word 'interesting' when they don't have anything positive to say, is that how you feel about the book?" or "Wow, I was so hoping you would see it as a way that I've carried on my parents' social justice legacy" or "Was there anything about the book you liked or learned from in any way?"

I shared Lily's reaction to the book with my friend Laura. I wasn't prepared for Lily's strong reluctance to talk about it. Laura thought Lily just didn't know what to say because incest is such a difficult topic for people to talk about. That surprised me, but as I thought about it I realized how taboo that topic was for people from my parents' generation.

As I spoke with Laura further, a deep well of pain came up as I realized how much I'd wanted my parents to be proud of my book.

***

I decided to call another of my parents' friends, Ronnie, to see what, if anything, she knew. We arranged to meet at a nearby restaurant.

I arrived first and found a table along the wall. The restaurant was dark, but there were candles on the table. She arrived and we both ordered wine. I needed to brace myself to broach the topic. I knew that this was the only way I'd have a chance to learn more about my parents and what they said or did during the years after they learned about my memories.

Ronnie and I went through the usual small talk. She asked about my daughter and I asked about hers. I waited until after we ordered and the food came so we wouldn't be interrupted. Once we were served, I bit the bullet. "Did you know that there'd been periods of time when I'd been estranged from my parents?" I asked.

Ronnie barely hesitated. "Yes, and your mother told me why."

I was taken aback. "Did my mother ever say how she felt about it?"

Ronnie looked straight at me. "Well," she said, "you know, your mother didn't do that."

I had to laugh and agree. My mother didn't talk about her feelings with me, but I wondered if she might have been different with some of her friends. Apparently, she wasn't. Ronnie didn't say any more during that conversation and I didn't press her. I thought I'd gone as far as I could.

A week or so later, I realized I had more questions for Ronnie. I hesitated before calling her, worried that she'd feel pressured or pushed, but I felt I had no choice. She picked up the phone and after greeting her, I immediately said, "Ronnie, I hope it's OK but there's something else I want to ask you."

"Go ahead," she said.

Forcing myself to be direct, I asked, "Could you tell me how my mother told you about...?"

Matter-of-factly, she responded, "Well, that was when Bernard [her husband] was still alive and we were in a restaurant. Your father was there, too. I asked your mother how you were doing and she told me that you had accused your father of sexually abusing you."

I couldn't believe that my mother had actually shared this with Ronnie and Bernard so directly and in such a public place. I was shocked. I had always assumed that my mother hadn't spoken to any of her friends about it because she'd have felt ashamed.

I took a deep breath and pushed myself to continue my inquiry. "Did my mother say anything else? Did my father say anything?"

Again without hesitation, Ronnie responded, "No, she didn't and your father didn't say anything either."

I probed further. "Did my mother make clear whether she believed me or not?"

"No, she never made that clear and I have no idea what she really believed, what she felt deep down. As your parents' friends though, Bernard and I had to assume it wasn't true. I know that Ann felt that there needed to be healing between you and them and that it was important to make whatever had happened to you as a child a part of the past."

Saddened and disappointed, I realized that everyone seemed to agree with my mother that it was best to "just forget the whole thing." Nonetheless, I was struck by her words, *"what she really believed, what she felt deep down"* and *"whatever happened to you as a child."* I thought Ronnie might have wondered if, on some level, my mother did believe me. I didn't have the courage to ask Ronnie what she herself believed. Feeling vulnerable, I didn't want to hear it if she did not.

Telling My Truth, Standing My Ground

***

I had coffee with my friend Laura soon after talking with Ronnie. She was among the first people I'd told about my memories back when I first retrieved them. Her mother had passed away years before my mother did. "Laura…did your mother ever say anything about what my mother said or felt during that time?"

"When you first told me about it, I mentioned it to my mother and she told me she'd heard about it from your mother, but she didn't say anything about what your mother actually said. She just said, 'Deborah is a strong girl,' which I took to mean that she completely believed you."

Laura's mother had known my mother since before I was born. Our families were close and she loved my mother and me. And, like Lily, she shared my parents' values and beliefs. Knowing that Laura's mother believed me meant a lot to me.

A few weeks later, I went down to Florida to visit Lily. I was determined, this time around, to ask all the questions I needed to ask and not hold myself back. Lily and Kay met me at the airport and we went back to Lily's house to drop off my luggage. Then, Kay and I went out to pick up some pizza for dinner. While we waited for the pizza, I told her about being molested by my father and talking to her mother about it. Kay was immediately supportive, and as I told her the whole story, she never once expressed doubt or surprise.

"What did my mother say when you told her?" Kay inquired.

Facing her, I tried to explain as best I could. "She said something about how people deny what they don't want to acknowledge."

Kay nodded. "Yeah, that doesn't surprise me. My father was abusive to all of us kids and my mother never did anything about it."

That came as a shock to me. "Really? I had no idea."

Here I was thinking my family was the only one with problems. Her father was a big man, spoke loudly, and had a biting tongue. As a child, I was always terrified to be around him. Nonetheless, the idea that he had been physically abusive to his children had never occurred to me.

Mystery of Memory

We went back to Lily's one-bedroom apartment. We ate together at a small table in the room that served as both living and dining room. Lily was in her nineties, but her brain was as sound as ever. Being with her felt like the closest thing to being with family that I had. Since my parents had passed away, my brother and I were the only ones left. We never had much of an extended family. I felt a combination of comfort, because I felt so at home with Lily, and discomfort because it was as if I'd come to visit her with a hidden agenda. I guess I had. Lily was one of the few people still alive who might be able to shed some light on my parents.

After dinner when Kay left, I asked, "So, Lily, what exactly did my mother say when she acknowledged that my father had molested me?"

Disappointingly, she backed off her story a little. "Oh, I think you misunderstood me. I wasn't saying that your mother acknowledged the truth of what happened, I remember your mother telling me that you were in therapy and made these accusations."

I was confused by what seemed like a change in Lily's account, but remained determined to probe further. "So what did she say about that? Did she say she believed me? Did she say she didn't believe me? Did she tell you what my father said to her about it?"

Lily replied, "She didn't say anything about whether or not she believed you or if your father said anything to her about it. I didn't ask any questions, because I felt it would be all guessing anyway, since your mother was a third party."

Disbelieving, I prodded, "Well, even if she was a third party, wouldn't she have told you, as a friend, what her husband told her about it, regardless of what she believed? How did she feel about the whole thing?"

"Well, you know," said Lily, "your mother and I were not really close at that time. It's true that we grew up together and went to school together from kindergarten through the end of high school, but in our college years, our lives went in different directions. Your mother went to live in Washington, DC after she graduated college. I got married and shortly after, Phil and I moved up to Maine."

I was shocked to hear Lily say that. I knew their paths had separated in some ways, but they definitely remained close. My family visited her family in Maine for many summers and after she retired to Florida, Lily regularly came to New York to visit my mother. She and my mother spoke on the phone regularly. In fact, she was the last person my mother spoke to on the phone before she passed away. I found it strange that Lily was trying to tell me that she and my mother weren't that close. Was she trying to convince me that she wasn't a good source of information about my mother so I'd stop asking questions?

Still wanting more information about my mother, I asked, "Lily, in all the years that you knew my mother, did you ever see her cry? Did she ever talk to you about her feelings?"

Without hesitating, she said, "No."

Lily echoed Ronnie's words. I had imagined that since Lily and my mother were such close friends, maybe it was different with her. I felt sad to think of my mother having no one with whom she was able to be vulnerable and express her emotions.

I told Lily how hurt I was that neither of my parents said anything to me about what they thought about my book after reading it.

"Well, did you ever ask them?" she inquired.

I hadn't. Strange as it sounds, when she said that, I realized if either of them had wanted to talk about the book with me, it probably would've been difficult for them to initiate the conversation.

A few months after I visited Lily and Kay in Florida, Kay called. I'd given her a copy of my book while I was in Florida. She told me she hadn't been able to bring herself to read it. She found it too painful to read about my father having done something to me. If it was painful for her to read, it gave me a sense of how difficult it may have been for my brother to do so. I'm embarrassed to admit that the idea never occurred to me before then.

***

Next, I called my mother's friend Thelma. After we exchanged greetings. I waited for a pause in the conversation and asked, "Thelma, can I ask you a difficult question?"

MYSTERY OF MEMORY

"Yes, you can."

"Did you know about the time when I wasn't in contact with my parents?" I asked.

"Yes, I do."

"Do you know why?"

In an irritated tone, she replied, "I don't like to remember such a long time ago. It wasn't pleasant."

"Did my mother ever speak to you about how she felt about it?" I asked.

Making it clear that she didn't want to talk about this with me, Thelma said, "C'mon Deborah, don't give me the third degree."

Clearly, I hit a sore spot, but I continued. "I'm sorry Thelma but you're one of the few people I can ask."

Sighing, she responded, "Human frailties are difficult to face and get over. My feeling is that all that is done, and you did the best you could, according to what you thought, and the way your parents communicated with you. And I think let bygones be bygones and not mull over it and over it because I don't think it gets further understanding."

It was the same thing my mother and Lily had said.

"Do you remember anything my mother said about her thoughts or feelings?"

"I don't think she expressed anything specific to me on that score," Thelma said.

"Well, if my daughter had told me what I had told my mother, I would've been worried about her and wanted to find a way to support her so I'm simply trying to understand my mother's reaction," I said.

"You can look at it in two ways: One, that it didn't happen, and two, that it happened and time has been a good healer, and that means that you put some of it away for future reference."

Before I could say anything else, her doorbell rang. She told me she had to go, but would call me back. She never did and passed away soon after.

After these conversations, I realized that, as opposed to my assumption that my parents would not have told anyone about my claims, my mother told many of her friends. This was a shock to me. Whether she believed me or not, I thought it was strange that my mother would share this information so publicly and without any indication of how she felt about me as a result. Despite how taboo the topic was for members of my mother's generation, she did not seem to be constrained by it.

***

I made one final call to one of my parents' friends, Esther. When I asked her if she knew that my parents and I had been out of communication for a number of years she said, "Yes, but I have no idea why. I always wondered about it. It wasn't something that they would talk about. Why are you asking?"

I told her the whole story. When I told her about my parents' calm reaction when Pierre told them about the sexual abuse, she said, "It's bizarre that neither of them expressed shock. I can't believe they didn't."

"So Esther, did my mother ever share her emotions or express her feelings to you?"

"Let me think. No, she was sort of...always the same, if you know what I mean. Your mother was kind of dry, non-committal, not very emotional."

We got off the phone after promising to get together soon. Fifteen minutes later Esther called back, "Debby, I feel terrible. I don't know why I did it, but I just lied to you. I did know why you weren't in communication with your parents.

I laughed.

"I'm so glad you're laughing because I expected you to be angry with me. Your parents didn't tell me about it. I heard it through the grapevine from one of our mutual friends. It was never discussed because it was too hot to handle. That topic was not talked about in those days. It was just too uncomfortable," she told me.

"So, what was the reaction among your group of friends?" I asked her.

"They all thought, "Debby's crazy."

It was painful to hear that, but not surprising since all of them had only heard my parents' side of the story. I imagined my mother leaning forward to talk in a low voice to her friends saying, "Well, she suffers from depression and when she went to see a therapist, he convinced her that she was molested as a child." Nonetheless, it was painful to hear how my parent's friends had reacted. These were all people who knew me since I was a child. Why was it so easy for them to assume something was wrong with me? I was cast as insane for telling my truth.

At the end of our conversation, she said, "Lying is so difficult. I felt terrible when I got off the phone with you."

I Learn More About My Parents

In addition to gathering data from my mother's friends, I also found information about my parents when cleaning out their papers after they died. I knew that my father had been married before he married my mother. When he spoke to me about his first marriage, he made it sound as if they were married for about six months, but when I found the divorce papers, I discovered that this was not the case. He got married in January of 1948 and separated in November of 1949. My father's divorce decree was granted in March of 1950 and my parents got married in December of that same year.

According to the divorce papers, his ex-wife, who had moved to Arkansas, filed for divorce on the grounds of "indignities to the person of the plaintiff, which being systematic and habitually pursued, rendered her condition in life intolerable."

I looked up the elements needed to prove a charge of indignities in Arkansas and found a number of definitions, although I couldn't be sure what the definition was in the 1940s. The descriptions I found included such words as rudeness, vulgarity, unmerited reproach, haughtiness, contempt, studied neglect, open insult, intentional incivility, injury, manifest disdain, abusive language, malignant ridicule, alienation, and estrangement.

Rudeness, open insult or malignant ridicule are not the kinds of things my father would have engaged in. I never saw him be intentionally rude or malicious to anyone. Abusive language? Cursing was not in my father's repertoire. The most I ever heard him say when angry was, "for Chrissake!!" or "For crying out loud!"

Vulgarity on the other hand, might fit. My father enjoyed pornography. In the last decade of his life, he viewed pornography on the Internet, particularly sites that involved women wrestling. After he passed away, I found black and white photos of scantily clad, athletic-looking women wrestling. As my father's Technical Support Help Desk, he once called because his computer screen froze and a weird message appeared kept coming up. Somehow, I helped him get rid of the problem. I mentioned it to friend of mine who laughed and explained he caught the same virus when logging onto some pornography sites. I wasn't surprised, therefore, when I visited my parents one day and my father called me into the study to ask how to delete his search history.

I told my friend Laura what I found and she shared with me some incidents involving my father that I didn't know about. She told me about an experience her older sister, Marsha, had with my father when she was about fourteen years old. Marsha had gotten her finger caught in a sliding door and was hospitalized. Since her parents didn't have a car, my father offered to pick her up when she was discharged. On the ride home, he offered to give her a massage. His offer disturbed Marsha and she told Laura about it.

She went on to tell me about an incident that occurred when we were about ten or so and I was away at summer camp. She and her parents had dinner at my parents' house. During the meal, my father talked about the fact that I was at a horseback-riding camp and wondered if the horses were "like a penis to the girls riding them." She remembers thinking how inappropriate it was that he made that kind of comment, particularly with her at the table. These stories were news to me and yet they weren't surprising.

***

Mystery of Memory

In the process of going through my parents' papers, I also found some of my father's unpublished writing. I imagined him sitting on his black desk chair, hunt-and-peck typing away on his Royal typewriter or in later years, his IBM Selectrix. Wearing one of his checked short-sleeved tailored shirts, he'd hunch over the keys as he wrote.

I discovered a piece of fiction he had written about two men, David and Arthur, who work in the advertising industry. David is still working while Arthur, his colleague, is retired. The piece starts with David about to meet Arthur for lunch. He is deliberating over whether or not to say anything to Arthur about having seen him leave a "porno shop" a few days earlier. David reminisces about how Arthur interviewed him for a job as copywriter at a Madison Avenue advertising agency. Having little confidence in his own writing, David feared the interview would be futile. Similar to David, my father had worked in small organizations as a writer and eventually, to his own surprise, at one of the major Madison Avenue advertising agencies.

When David entered Arthur's office, he admired a drawing on the wall, which Arthur told him was, "an early David Levine." Artist and caricaturist David Levine was a close friend of my parents and a number of his drawings hung in our home. My father probably had at least one in his Madison Avenue office.

Despite David's misgivings, the job interview turned into a spirited discussion on writing and philosophy. Both men shared their love of books and specific writers. During their discussion, Arthur said, "Miword! [sic] You're the first guy I've met in years who has read Nexo. Martin Anderson Nexo, one of the great radical writers. Have you read *Independent People* by Halldor Laxness? He's a lot like Nexo."

David was hired. Like both David and Arthur, my father loved discussions about books and writers and the expression Arthur used, "My word" was one my father used all the time. The more I read, the more parallels I saw.

At this point we learn that Arthur is worried about David having seen him exit the porn shop.

Telling My Truth, Standing My Ground

It was a secret Arthur had lived with as long as he could recall. He could not remember when 'it' had first occupied his mind, but then he could not remember much of what happened in his life before he was twelve. Perhaps there had been some traumatic event that occurred during those earlier, formative years, years he could only barely recall as long, dim, empty corridors in his memory.

As with Arthur, my father had few memories of his own childhood. The wording in this piece was almost identical to a short autobiographical piece I also found with his writing drafts.

Coupled with my father experiencing the same difficulty recalling childhood memories as me, all this seemed as if it was more than mere coincidence. Going through my father's personal writing, I felt like a spy stealthily reading through what might be considered private material, yet, I also felt like a detective looking for whatever clues I could find about him. Reading this paragraph about a possible "traumatic event," I thought I'd hit the mother lode.

The piece continues alluding to the hidden compulsion that led Arthur to search through the pornography stores in Times Square "looking for photographs, articles, drawings, cartoons, stories of anything that pictured, promised or in any way suggested the things he hoped to find." (Contrary to the Disney-like atmosphere of Times Square today, in those days it was the center of pornography stores and movie theatres.) He ended up going into therapy, but was told it would require deeper, costlier analysis to find out the source of the obsession.

The writing doesn't contain any details about what Arthur's hidden obsession was. All I was left with was the knowledge that visiting porn shops was the only way Arthur was able to quench his secret desire. What was Arthur's (or my father's) "compulsion"? It appears to have been sexual, but if my father's compulsion were simply looking at pictures of nearly naked athletic women wrestlers, I don't think he would have felt the need to seek professional help for it. Might whatever this compulsion was, have been the basis of his divorce on the grounds of "indignities"?

Mystery of Memory

***

Years later, in a casual conversation with a family friend who had known my father since before he was married, I learned that when my father was young, his family, unable to afford rent, ended up living with his Uncle Sam, his mother's brother. Uncle Sam was an architect who owned a house in Manhattan. He invited my grandparents and my father and his sister to come live in his home. Sam gave the master bedroom to my grandparents and he and my father shared a bedroom, sleeping in the same bed.

During that period—it must've been the late 1920s or early 1930s—it wasn't unheard of for adults and children to share beds in tenement apartments when there was no place else to sleep, but this wasn't a tenement. I wondered what kind of relationship my father had with his Uncle Sam. I know that my father was closer with his uncle than his own father. Uncle Sam passed away when I was in high school. When my father told my brother and me, he was in tears and barely able to speak. I witnessed no such emotion when his father passed away, a number of years later. In a short autobiographical piece, my father described his father.

He was not the kind of man who invited confidences or offered advice. If there had ever been an opportunity to talk, father to son, he never took advantage of it. There was no question that he loved his family, but my father was satisfied to leave the bringing up of his children almost entirely to my mother.

I always had the sense that my father received affection from his uncle that he didn't get from his own father. If Uncle Sam abused my father, it's possible that my father repressed the memories of what happened to him, as he repressed whatever he did to me. If so, perhaps my father's hyperactivity and need for control were coping mechanisms.

I saw that pattern in myself, but it was only after I started therapy that I became aware of this tendency. I found a diary entry from when I decided I wanted to get pregnant.

There's an empty place under the freneticism that I need to acknowledge—the part of me that feels she'll be left in the cold and unattended to if I have a baby. I almost feel as if I'm deluding myself—jumping into a fantasy land about how easy it'll be— running so fast so I won't stop and think and be scared and change my mind. I need to find out what the tired, empty, unknown place in my chest is.

People run away from their feelings all the time. Some people turn to alcohol or drugs, others become workaholics, still others play videogames non-stop. Maybe my father's constant motion was his way of running from his thoughts and feelings, as my mother's stoic lack of warmth and emotion might have been her way of keeping hers at bay.

***

I knew little about my mother's childhood, but I did wonder why she kept her emotions completely bottled up. Through her entire adulthood, my aunt Joan complained bitterly that my mother was the favorite child. Could it be that the "special treatment" my aunt had long resented was in actuality unwanted sexual attention? Was this why my mother was so devoid of emotions? Could she be like the mother in the *Scared Silent* documentary who had been sexually molested as a child?

I learned more about my mother in the process of sorting through my parents' belongings. In addition to the photo albums with pictures of my nuclear family, my parents had numerous photos from each of their childhoods. I wanted digital copies of all the photos, but didn't want the albums themselves. I went through the time-consuming process of scanning all the pictures. I didn't really look at them in the process, figuring I could review and organize them once I had finished and given the albums to my brother.

A few months later, I decided to start organizing the pictures. I came across a photo of my mother and her sister standing stark naked in the doorway of what looks to be a cabin they stayed in when they vacationed in Martha's Vineyard.

Mystery of Memory

My mother was about twelve years old and Joan was about ten. They are both pre-pubescent with no pubic hair and undeveloped breasts. In addition, they are clearly posed and not happy to have their picture taken.

Three wooden steps lead up to a wood-framed doorway where they stand; a screen door behind them. The walls of the cabin are octagonal shingles. My mother is on the left, with a huge rustic-looking wooden door swung completely open on her right side. My aunt is on the right, her left hand grasping a towel hanging from a hook. An upside-down mop leans against the cabin wall. It appears to be mid-day. There is no shade so they are completely exposed to the harsh sunlight.

My mother's body faces forward, her arms hanging at her sides. She leans slightly on the doorjamb, the whole of her right arm touching it. Her eyes, however, are directed to her right. My aunt stands with her body turned in the same direction my mother looks, her left buttock against her side of the doorjamb. They both appear to be looking at whoever is taking the picture—most likely my grandfather, known in our family for his photography.

In the photo, my mother's hair is just below shoulder length. Her face is tight; her lips neither smiling nor frowning. My aunt's hair is shorter, her chin is down and her eyebrows furrowed. My mother looks scared and my aunt looks angry.

***

My chest tightened as I looked at this picture. I felt like I was invading my mother and her sister's privacy, violating them by being a witness to what I imagine was a humiliating experience for them.

Shortly after finding this photo, I went out for coffee with Laura. I wanted to show her the photo to see if I was reading too much into it. She looked at it briefly and said, "Deb, if this picture were developed in a photo shop in this day and age, it would be reported as child pornography."

***

Something else I found among my parents' belongings were their copies of *Repairing the Quilt of Humanity*. Neither of the spines appeared bent, nor did any of the pages looked dog-eared. I was baffled. Had they read my book? If they hadn't, why did they keep the copies?

Of my parents' possessions, I only took a few items: some of my mother's jewelry and some dishes. A friend of my parents had painted portraits of each of them. I wanted the portrait of my mother; it captures the essence of who she was—elegant, cool and beautiful. Her ice blue tailored shirt and silver earrings bring out the beauty of her blue eyes and silver hair. Her energy is calm, almost regal. I love that painting.

I was ambivalent, however, about hanging my father's portrait in my home. There's an energy emanating from his eyes that might seem mischievous to some, but for me seems lecherous as well. It's similar to an optical illusion image in which, depending on your focus, you can see two different faces. In the end, I brought it home, because my daughter wanted me to take it.

I hung the portraits side by side on the wall leading from the dining room in the front area of my apartment to the living room/office in the back. I sat at my desk one day thinking about these pictures. I stood up, walked around my long black desk to stand in front of my father's portrait. I saw the twinkle in his right eye and the smile starting to emerge, but within milliseconds, a congested heaviness took over my chest and tears rolled down my face. My father's eyes seemed menacing. I started sobbing. Over the years, I came to forgive and love him deeply, but looking at that portrait sparked a deep-seated sadness of how I wished things had been different. When I repainted my apartment a few years later, I took the portraits down.

VI. Telling My Truth, Standing My Ground

I Talk With My Brother

Shortly after going through my parents' papers, I participated in *The Art of Transformative Consulting,* a weeklong program in Washington, DC. It was an experiential, interactive experience designed for consultants working to create social change. Much of the work was done in pairs and small groups. One exercise was to role-play having a "courageous conversation"—one with someone to whom you are afraid to speak. It's a conversation in which you take the risk of dealing with another in an authentic, direct way, creating space for both individuals to share their thoughts and feelings.

I decided to use this opportunity to practice having a conversation with my brother about our relationship, which I had been avoiding for years. My partner in this exercise, a woman, played the role of my brother. Without reflecting on what I wanted to say or telling my partner anything about the content of the conversation, I dove in. "Aaron, I don't know why you never talked to me about what I told you Daddy did to me. I can't believe that when I came to New York after writing to you about it, the only thing you did was ask me why I dated black men."

As those words came out of my mouth, I experienced a deep sense of hurt that I had not tapped into up until then. Tears fell down my face. "Why weren't you there to support me? I needed you to be there for me."

My partner simply replied, "I don't know what you want me to say."

Hearing this woman who knew nothing about the situation say those words from a place of heartfelt sincerity opened my eyes to a wider perspective. Through all my years of avoiding this topic with my brother, I hadn't been able to imagine what it must have been like for him. I saw that, whether my brother believed me or not, he probably had no idea what to say to me. I was so scared for so long it blinded me to how my brother must have felt. I was even beginning to understand my parents wanting to forget about the whole thing. I didn't like what happened, I wished it had been different, but I was developing empathy and compassion for them.

I now understood why, when my parents visited me in Japan, they looked shocked when I was angry at them for not talking about the molestation. I had given them no reason to believe I planned to ever bring the topic up again. When my father tried to talk to me about the impact on me of what he'd done when we had lunch together in New York, I ended the conversation telling him I had just needed to hear him acknowledge that it happened. When I made demands on them to talk with me about it, I was, in effect, changing the rules. First it was, "All I needed is to have some closure," and then all of a sudden, it became, "How can you simply go on as if nothing ever happened?"

What could they say?

From that simple role-play, I came to understand a number of things. I was deeply hurt that my brother never reached out to me when I was estranged from my parents. I had been too scared to approach him about it. I didn't think I'd be able to bear the pain of opening up that wound and getting in touch with the pain, sense of betrayal and loneliness that would come if he rejected my overture. I decided

I needed to have a discussion with him about the things we had never spoken about. I called him and invited him to dinner.

Coincidentally, on the morning of the day I was to meet my brother, I had one of my monthly calls with two friends, Bert and James. I met these two men at the *Art of Transformative Consulting* workshop. We'd worked together in a number of exercises during the program and agreed to talk on a regular basis to help each other in our ongoing personal growth and development.

"Well, I finally scheduled dinner to talk things over with my brother," I told them.

"Deb, that's great. I know it must be a difficult situation for you," said James.

"Have you ever talked with your brother about your being molested?" asked Bert.

I told them how I had written a letter to my brother decades before, how he called and we agreed to talk in person when I was next in New York.

"Before I tell you what happened in that conversation, I'm curious to hear from you. If you were my brother, what do you think you would have said to me?"

"I would probably respond with some kind of empathy and recognition of the pain you were going through. I'd tell you how sorry I was that this happened to you. I'd probably stumble because I wouldn't know what to make of it. Maybe I would've said, 'I don't know what to make of this. It's hard to believe. It seems so unreal, it doesn't make sense,'" said James.

"What if you didn't believe it? Then, what would you say?" I asked.

Laughing, Bert said, "Can you prove it?"

I told them about our conversation and how almost as soon as we started talking, my brother asked me why I always dated black men.

"I didn't see that coming," said Bert.

"So, what do you think you would have said in response to that question if you were me?"

Laughing, Bert immediately said: "What the fuck are you talking about?"

Funny as Bert's reaction was, in hearing it, I thought that perhaps my own reaction had been a bit bizarre. Not only did I not get angry, I don't even remember trying to bring the conversation back on topic.

"Looking back at it, I think I was either too scared of rejection or maybe I was just relieved that he didn't cross-examine me or call me a liar," I said. "And while I didn't think about it then, I also I realize there's a possibility that he was molested as well," I added tentatively.

"I wasn't going to say that, but that might be a reason he hasn't wanted to talk about it." Bert said.

"Well, what do you want to have happen at dinner with your brother tonight? Imagine yourself having this talk with your brother. What would each of you need? What does the conversation need to look like? How can you shape it so you can both have a healthy and productive conversation?" James asked.

"I want a more authentic relationship with him. I want to be connected with him instead of feeling the need to defend myself from him," I said.

***

I'd been able to have conversations with friends of my parents that I was never able to have before because I had been protecting my parents. In the case of my brother, not reaching out was about self-protection. After getting off the phone with Bert and James, I pondered the questions I wanted to ask Aaron: What happened that resulted in us becoming estranged when I was not communicating with our parents? Why hadn't he ever reached out to me? Why did he never talk to me about *Repairing the Quilt of Humanity*?

Later in the day, I had a moment of panic. As I imagined speaking with my brother, my heart raced. My chest tightened as I considered that now that our parents had passed away, my brother and I are the only ones remaining from our immediate family. I was afraid of losing him. What if he feels hurt or ambushed? What if he gets angry and rejects me? Maybe I should just leave it alone—it's all in the past after all. I forced myself to go forward, because larger than my fear was my desire to re-connect with him on an authentic level.

We went to a restaurant two blocks from my home. We sat at a table for two in the corner. My brother, who always dresses casually, was wearing jeans and a T-shirt. His straight dirty blond hair was scattered with gray and fairly short, but not as short as a crew cut. We sat across from each other, my back against the wall.

I was determined to broach the topic before we ordered food— maybe over drinks, but I wasn't able to find an opening. Finally, as we ate, I began. "I want to talk with you about something, but if you don't want to it's OK. I'm not trying to force anything, but I would like to talk to you about our relationship and ask you some questions."

"Sure, go ahead," he said without any note of defensiveness or hesitation.

"I never understood why, when I was estranged from Mom and Da, you and I stopped talking. What happened?"

"You got angry at me because I wasn't willing to take sides."

"Wow, I don't remember saying that to you." After we both took that in, I went on. "Another thing I wondered is why, when we met in your office for the first time after I'd written to you about the incest, the only thing you asked me was why I dated black men."

"I don't remember saying that. If I did, it was probably because I had no idea what to say, so I asked the first stupid question that popped into my mind."

For years I'd been so angry and disappointed about this incident, but hearing him say that so matter-of-factly made complete sense to me. I realized he might actually have said he didn't know what to say, and went on to ask that inane question, but that question was the only part of the conversation that I remembered.

I was fascinated by how differently we remembered the same events. My fears turned out to be unfounded.

"Well, do you remember how neither of the folks recognized me at Grandpa's funeral?"

"No, I don't."

"It's possible that you didn't witness either instance."

"I remember you having lunch with Sarah and telling her to, 'run away from me as fast as possible.'"

"I never said that. Do you want to know what really happened?"

"Yes."

"Sarah invited me over to lunch once. This was before I stopped communicating with the folks. Out of the blue, she asked me if the two of you had children, did I think she should worry about leaving the children alone with 'him'? I thought she meant Da, and told her as long as Mom was around I wouldn't worry about it. Then I realized she was talking about you. I had never considered that before but told her it was worth thinking about since incest can repeat across generations. Then, later she said something about how she's just like Mom—they both turn their emotions into Martinis."

"The two of them did like to drink Martinis together," he said.

"I never told Sarah to run away from you. But that may be how she interpreted a letter I sent to her a few years after. When Michael was about two years old, I woke up one morning with a sense of fear on his behalf—he was around the same age I was when Da molested me. I never accused you of anything and I never said or thought anything malicious about you. When I wrote it, I was…"

Finishing my sentence, he said "…doing it because you cared."

I sensed that no matter what he might have thought at that time, he now understood my motive and wasn't angry or hurt.

"What about the time the family sent Sarah to talk with me about my being 'depressed' and to tell me Mom was worried about the 'quality of men' I dated?"

"I don't remember that at all."

After a short pause, he said, "Dad would have cut off his arm for you. He went to a doctor and took sodium pentothal to try to find out if something happened."

Mystery of Memory

Reviewing this conversation later, I realized that my brother's intent when telling me about my father taking sodium pentothal, was his way of telling me how much my father would sacrifice for me. At the time, however, I defensively interpreted it as my father selfishly wanting to prove himself innocent. That's why I followed up with a question trying to determine what else my father told him.

"Well, did Daddy ever tell you that we went to see a psychiatrist in New York?"

"No."

"We both met with a psychiatrist while I was in town for your wedding. In the meeting, I shared my memories and he listened. Then, at the end of the session, after we walked into the waiting room, he hugged me and with tears in his eyes, said he had no memory of any of it, but he must have done something and he apologized.

"I didn't know that. He probably just said something like that to make you feel better."

"Well, then why did he say something again that same week? We were in a restaurant and I didn't bring up the topic. He did. He asked me, again with tears in his eyes, if he had ruined my life."

He seemed surprised when I told him that. Then I broached the subject of my book, *Repairing the Quilt of Humanity*. "I remember once asking you about what you thought about the book and you either said, 'I didn't read it because I'd rather keep my head in the sand' or "Well, if you don't have anything nice to say…'"

"I looked it over, but I found reading the book too bizarre. I couldn't reconcile the dedication you wrote with the incest," he replied.

"I meant what I wrote in the dedication. I'm grateful for the social justice legacy and the values they left me. Also, I wanted to protect Da and not expose him in any way. I purposely wrote it so that anyone reading it would probably assume the perpetrator was an uncle."

I guess just as I'd had difficulty coming to terms with accepting that my parents can be both wonderful and capable of hurting me deeply, it was challenging for him to accept that I could write the book holding the paradox of both those realities. Then I asked him the question that lingered in the back of my mind. "Do you think there is any possibility that Daddy molested you as well?"

"No, not at all." He sounded clear and certain in his response.

"So why do you think you threatened suicide when you were in junior high school?"

"I threatened suicide because I hated school and I hated my life. I was miserable because I had no friends."

"Do you remember seeing a psychiatrist at that time? I remember the time we all went to see a psychiatrist as a family."

"I don't remember that. I remember going to see Dr. Chess. I couldn't stand her. She couldn't get anything out of me." This was the same psychiatrist I'd been sent to when I had been so disturbed after seeing *The Exorcist*. We seemed to have had similar experiences with and reactions to her. The psychiatrist I remember the family going to see, however, was male. I didn't think to mention it then.

What was beautiful about this meeting was that neither of us was defensive. We were both open and curious, and even had a sense of humor about it. Only once in the conversation did his voice have a bit of an edge. This was when he talked about my parents' reaction when I returned from a youth leadership program I had attended in Colorado the summer after my sophomore year in high school. This program was designed to bring together teenagers from a variety of racial, ethnic, socio-economic and geographic backgrounds to create our own community and engage in service work in the outside community.

That experience was life-changing. Through it, I had my first introduction to the U.S. prison system. We visited prisons and met ex-convicts from the Fortune Society (a prison reform organization in New York City) who talked about their experiences. I also remember lengthy discussions about issues of race and injustice. This was probably my first experience developing close friendships with individuals from entirely different socio-economic backgrounds. A large group of participants had come from North Philadelphia, which at least in the late 1970s, was considered a ghetto.

"When you came back from that program, the folks felt used because you returned from it with extreme white guilt. The program really messed with you."

"What do you mean? How did they feel used?"

"You came out with some stuff about how they had to have people stay over."

"I remember asking the folks if my friends from the program who lived in Philadelphia could stay with us so they could attend the program's alumni reunion in New York City that fall." I have a vague memory of my parents trying to say that we didn't have enough room to host them, but that argument didn't hold since all of us could sleep on the living room floor in sleeping bags. In any event, they agreed in the end.

"If the program was so terrible, why did they send me back the next summer as a staff member?" I asked.

"I don't know, but they felt used. You returned with white guilt and that was crazy given the folks' background. They supported civil rights. Dad wrote promotional materials for every negro organization there was."

I was so surprised to hear what he was saying that I didn't even react when he used the word, "negro." Was he saying that my having white guilt was the equivalent of accusing my parents of racism? I asked, "Given their background, why would Ma quiz me about the color of the skin of my friends or tell Laura that she was concerned that I was dating black men?"

He agreed that it was strange of our mother to have acted that way. This was the only point in the entire conversation where I sensed any defensiveness or even anger in his tone. Why did that summer leadership program experience make my parents, and perhaps my brother, so uncomfortable? Maybe I accused my parents of being hypocrites?

Finally, I showed him a copy of the nude photo of our mother and Joan. "This is a picture I found of Mom and Joan when I was scanning all the family photos. I want to get your reaction to it."

"Wow, they both look unhappy and scared," he said.

"Do you agree that it would count as child pornography by today's standards?"

"Yes. Well, Lily once told me that Grandpa Saul used to yell and lose his temper."

That was as far as our conversation went. I didn't ask him how our grandfather's yelling had anything to do with our mother and aunt naked in the photo. Simply broaching the topic with my brother was a huge success. It wasn't until afterwards, however, that I realized I hadn't shared any of my feelings with him. I never told him how hurtful it was to be estranged from the family or how much I wish he had supported me during those years. When I think about it, I can't think of any instances when I shared feelings of hurt with any member of my family. Anger yes, pain, no.

The next day I shared this experience with a friend of mine. As I was telling him how well the dinner had gone and that I knew that my brother knows I love him, tears came to my eyes. For years, I hadn't allowed myself to admit how much I love my brother and want his love. Then, moments later, the fear came along with tightness in my chest. What will happen when he reads this book? Are there some things I need to change so I won't hurt, anger or humiliate him?

The "Great Incest War"

As part of my investigation while writing this book, I did research on incest, trauma and memory, and learned about what was known as the "Great Incest War." I didn't know about it at the time, but it happened right about when my father had recanted. This "war" was between those who believe that individuals may repress memories of childhood incest and recover them later in life, and supporters of the "False Memory Movement," who consider repressed memories of incest to be a myth.

Mystery of Memory

Supporters of the Movement believe "memory recovery therapy," such as hypnosis, guided imagery, relaxation techniques, and the use of sedatives, can create false memories. They contend that many therapists use suggestion, coercion and manipulation and as a result, their patients develop false memories.

I searched for books and articles on both sides. I discovered that the originators of the False Memory Movement were Pamela and Peter Freyd, a couple whose daughter Jennifer, a professor of psychology at the University of Oregon, had accused Peter of sexually abusing her as a child. They established the False Memory Foundation (whose members consists mainly of parents whose children have accused them of abuse) and coined the term "False Memory Syndrome," for claims of childhood abuse based on memories recovered by adults.

I wondered if my father's recanting came from learning about this False Memory Movement. After all, he'd said during our phone call on Mother's Day, "Your therapist fucked you up. I never did anything to you."

Prior to beginning my research, I knew that a group of some kind contested the veracity of recovered memories of sexual abuse. I was horrified to read about the way Jennifer Freyd's parents publicly attacked her. Calling herself Jane Doe, Jennifer's mother, Pamela, wrote about Jennifer's accusations in a journal that focused on false accusations of childhood sexual abuse. She then circulated the article, including personal and professional information about Jennifer, to Jennifer's colleagues and to the media. For years, I feared being seen as crazy by my parents; now I worried that someone from the False Memory Movement would publicly attack me if I wrote about being molested by my father. They'd claim that nothing had happened, that my therapist had "planted" the memories in my mind.

I cringed when I saw an article on the Internet that endorsed Bill Cosby's innocence by maligning each of the women who had accused him of sexual assault. People found it impossible to believe that the charming Bill Cosby of pudding commercials or Cliff Huxtable, father of the perfect family, could have sexually assaulted anyone. They would find it just as impossible to believe that a solid citizen like my father could have molested me.

The more I looked, the more I saw victims of sexual abuse maligned by society and treated as crazy unless overwhelming evidence proved otherwise. The movie *Spotlight*, which focused on the investigation of accusations of sexual abuse by Catholic priests, made this abundantly clear. Until devastating evidence surfaced, reporters thought one of the victims, who originally brought the story to the *Boston Globe*, was crazy. The idea of opening myself to attack from people who might try to discredit me for writing about my own experience was terrifying.

This is the cruel bind in which many incest survivors attempting to share their truth are placed. If they claim incest as the root cause of symptoms of depression, shame, fear, etc., they are accused of "playing the false memory card," the way people of color are accused of "playing the race card," whenever they bring up race as a possible factor in certain situations. In both cases, the group whose interpretation of reality is denied and discredited is the group that has a subordinated position in society. What's bizarre in both cases is that the "card" we are supposedly playing is never a winning card.

Invalidating and discrediting members of subordinated groups in society is part of U.S. culture. It's visible in the way white police officers who assault black men, women and children are excused. This societal denial takes place even in the face of videotaped evidence of police brutality and unwarranted violence.

I was relieved when I discovered numerous incidents in which recovered memories had been corroborated. Ross Cheit, a professor of Political Science at Brown University, had surfaced memories of sexual abuse at a summer camp he attended three decades before. The perpetrator, someone who Cheit had admired and trusted, confessed when confronted. Cheit concluded that his admiration for the abuser kept him from remembering that he had been molested.

I also found a study conducted by Dr. Linda M. Williams, Professor of Criminal Justice and Criminology at the University of Massachusetts. She interviewed women with documented histories of child sexual abuse, almost twenty years after their victimization took place. More than a third of them had no memories of their abuse; women who had been younger at the time of the incident, and those molested by someone they knew, were more likely to have no recall.

The two trauma experts whose work resonated most with me were Dr. Bessel van der Kolk, author of *The Body Keeps the Score,* and Judith Herman, author of *Trauma and Recovery: The Aftermath of Violence—From Domestic Abuse to Political Terror*. Van der Kolk explains that memories of traumatic experiences, unlike normal memories, are not organized as coherent logical narratives, but rather in "fragmented sensory and emotional traces." In a study he conducted, the narratives of participants who had been abused as children were the most fragmented; their memories arrived as images, physical sensations, sounds and intense emotions.

This describes my experience to a tee. Other than the two memories I recovered under hypnosis, I haven't been able to retrieve any others. However, I realize I have experienced the fragmented sensory traces Van der Kolk describes. For example, there were times when I was having sex when I was married that I had flashes of my father on top of me. At those times, I had to open my eyes to see that I was with Jeffrey, not my father. It never occurred to me that those flashes constituted memories until, while writing this book, a friend of mine asked me why not. At first, I rejected that possibility out of hand. But when he continued to question me and I forced myself to consider what these fragmentary images might mean, tears came to my eyes, my chest felt tense, and I could sense a well of grief held in check. I realized these flashing images were not coming out of thin air; they were triggered by the physical act of having sex. Hard as it was for me to believe that my father had fondled me as a child, it was almost unbearable for me to consider that he had had sexual intercourse with me. Not allowing myself to see these images as memories was my way of protecting myself from seeing my father as an abuser and protecting my father as well. Truly acknowledging the abuse felt like a betrayal of my father. This makes sense based on what Herman describes as the way abused children develop mechanisms to preserve their relationships with their parents. These psychological defenses include keeping the experiences outside their conscious awareness, and minimizing, rationalizing or excusing their abuse. It's easier for me to see my father as a man who experienced sexual abuse as a child, who "molested" me and then repressed all memory of it, than to see him as someone who "abused" and actually raped me. Confronting that reality is unbearably painful.

My Body Tells the Story

I had another transformative experience during the weeklong *Art of Transformative Consulting* program. Through it, I completely understood what Audre Lourde meant when she wrote, "We recognize that all knowledge is mediated through the body and that feeling is a profound source of information about our lives."

At least once each day, the trainer, Robert Gass, asked for volunteers so he could demonstrate skills and practices he was teaching. On the next-to-last day, Gass asked all of us to come up with an affirmation for ourselves to frame how we do our consulting work. Then he asked for a volunteer for a demonstration of how to ground and integrate our affirmations. I stepped forward. My affirmation was, "I boldly step into my powerful energy."

After working with me to slightly modify the wording, he asked, "What are the 'secondary voices' inside you saying." In other words, he was asking what voices of doubt I heard inside my head when I stated my affirmation. The first words that came out of my mouth were, "Are you kidding me?"

"Can you say more?" he asked.

"My throat is tightening and closing up," I said.

"Ok, just focus on your throat and allow it to be tight. Now what do the voices say?"

"You can't say that!"

"What can't you say?"

For a short while, no words came out, but tears were pouring down my face. While my throat had tightened in this past, this time it was so constricted I couldn't speak. All I could do was stare helplessly at Gass. Finally, the words that came out were, "That my father molested me."

My body became heavy, as if it were being sucked or pulled down through the chair into the ground. I was so weighted down that couldn't have stood up if I tried. My body was completely numb. I was slipping away—I felt myself almost disappearing.

I know the main defense mechanisms my body uses to keep feelings and memories repressed and hidden are my throat tightening, my body going numb or going to sleep. My throat kept me from speaking words that would have put me in danger as a child. To keep me from re-experiencing painful memories, my body becomes numb, or I enter a trance-like, dissociative state. In this case, these sensations were stronger than they had ever been. Finally, I was able to tell Gass, "I feel completely numb."

"Well, that seems like a smart thing to do," he replied.

At this point, I was sobbing as I said, "The problem isn't saying that my father molested me, it's believing myself when I say it."

"OK, try saying, 'Even if I don't believe myself, even if I'm not perfect, even if I doubt myself, I step into my power.'" The numbness began to dissipate as I repeated those words and listened to Gass say, "Do you have to 'step into' your powerful energy? Even that seems like too much work."

"It could be, 'I open into my powerful energy,'" I said as the tears subsided.

"What about relax into my full power?" When he said that, my chest tightened and I said, "If I relax, how can I protect myself? How can I protect myself if I am not aggressive or mean?"

He laughed. "Why can't you be mean?" he asked and had me repeat, "Even if I'm mean and not perfect, I relax into my full power."

As I said those words, the tightness and numbness dissolved and my throat, chest and heart felt light and open. My body felt empty, cleansed and in complete integrity with myself. I left that day feeling completely grounded.

At a somatic and emotional level, I knew I had been molested. My self-doubt lifted; the last piece of the puzzle had fallen into place.

From Forgiveness to Empathy

I had long since forgiven my parents and was able to feel some compassion for them. What I didn't realize until much later was that there is a feeling beyond forgiveness: empathy. I wasn't ready for that before. Through the process of writing this book, I tried to put myself in my parents' shoes. I developed empathy for them and could see them as more whole human beings with human frailties, who simply did the best they could. I came to understand that both of my parents loved me the only way they knew how.

***

Coming to better understand my parents helped me better understand my daughter. Maya and I had some pretty rough years when she was in high school. Like me, she suffers from depression but while I turn it inwards against myself, she turned it outward into anger. She expressed feelings of rage; I experienced her outbursts as attacks and closed down, becoming emotionally numb. My daughter accused me of being an "ice queen." Walls came down over my chest to protect my heart. This made sense as an adaptive response in childhood where it was not safe to expose my heart. But my capacity to empathize and be warm disappeared—I couldn't feel compassion once I closed my heart. I couldn't sense the pain and hurt underneath my daughter's rage.

At these times, I didn't feel like myself. Eerily, I felt like my mother. My posture stiffened and my facial expression became blank.

Mystery of Memory

I thought if I looked in a mirror in those moments, I would resemble my mother. This disturbed me—I had always prided myself on not being cold like her. But as I experienced myself shutting down, I had a better understanding of both my daughter and my parents. I could see myself in my daughter as she raged against me and called me unfeeling. I came to understand that her anger, like mine against my parents, was a cover for the depth of pain and vulnerability she was experiencing.

Seeing myself become my mother in the face of my daughter's emotions enabled me to truly understand how my parents may have experienced me. Where I saw myself reaching out and exposing my pain and hurt, all they could see and feel was my anger and combative tone, leaving them feeling the need to defend themselves. Their defenses went up to keep them from feeling my rage. Perhaps they were defending themselves from acknowledging a painful truth as well. Having come to understand how taboo the topic of incest is for my parents' generation, I can see how much more reason they would have to keep any memories repressed. Being emotionally caught up in protecting themselves and repressing their own emotions, they couldn't even begin to access any compassion for me.

I shut down when my daughter was enraged, partly because I felt stuck. If I apologized, she wouldn't accept my apology. If I didn't apologize, she was furious. If I attempted to hold her, she would push me away. If I didn't reach out to hold her, she accused me of being cold and uncaring. I would ask her over and over, "Baby, what can I do to help you feel better?"

Like my mother, I am capable of shutting down emotionally. But I came to understand that by bringing down a wall to keep hurt out, it also kept my compassion locked up as well. In the process of protecting myself, I wasn't able to allow my heart to open to my daughter's pain. I needed to re-train myself so that this was not my default response. Now, when I sense the walls come down in interactions with my daughter, I catch myself and intentionally focus on keeping my heart open.

Protecting myself by being numb is easy. What is most challenging and takes the most courage for me is to consciously keep my heart open in the face of the anger of the person I love most.

My daughter is among the most loving people I know. When I think about the sources of her anger, I can come up with a variety of possibilities in addition to her depression: her feeling abandoned when her father and I got divorced when she was four years old; my difficulty dealing with anger, making it difficult for her to express her feelings appropriately. I also believe that the trauma I experienced as a child was passed on to her at a cellular level.

***

When I started writing this book, I had no idea that I would be able to move from self-doubt to clarity. More surprising to me than the clarity I gained through this journey was that I was also able to move from forgiveness to empathy for my parents. To do this, I had to overcome my own fear and sense of powerlessness. As long as I remained in fear, I couldn't be open to my parents' feelings and the knowledge that they both loved me deeply. For years, vulnerability kept me blind to the pain, confusion, fear and hurt that my parents must have been feeling. I was unable to believe in and receive their love. Being able to do this involved tapping into my own sense of personal power. I also had to accept the paradoxes of reality. The both/and nature of life and human beings: that my parents could both love and hurt me; that I could be intimidating to my parents even if I was feeling small, powerless and helpless; that my parents and I could be both wonderful, loving people and capable of hurtful and cruel actions.

Some of this insight is also the result of my own experiences raising Maya. Seeing both my best and worse selves in my relationship with her brought home the understanding of how important it is to neither deify nor vilify others. We are all capable of both what's evil and what's divine.

What I know now is that for me to be healed and whole, and to be a conduit of divine energy on behalf of my family, friends and clients,

I need to be able to keep my heart open, even in the face of anger and fear.

TELLING MY TRUTH, STANDING MY GROUND

I'll never know exactly what happened to me or for how long. My body tells me clearly that I had an early childhood experience of being sexually violated and betrayed, one that left me with a crippling sense of self-doubt. This experience impacted my entire life: who I am, what I do, what I believe and what I feel.

Taking a journey into the pain of my own self-doubt and facing it head-on is how I've come through on the other side, clear and confident in trusting my own reality. I came to understand that my inability to be certain about what happened is part of the damage of the abuse itself. I had to reach the point at which I could give credibility to the intuitive and somatic ways my body has been telling me its truth for years.

I wasn't able to write this book while my parents were living. I can't even imagine how they would've reacted—whenever I try, all I can see is the two of them in pain. I never wanted to hurt my parents. Who am I to make them face what they might have been too scared to look at? Now that I have conquered my own self-doubt, I no longer have the need for their validation. We all have our own demons to face and we have to face them in our own time, in our own space. I am content knowing that my parents did the best they could with what they had.

I realize how far I've come from the day I decided to write this book. This journey was possible not because I searched for external validation, but because I went deep inside myself for the answers. Instead of battling forever with my parents, I set aside my fight to journey into myself. What I have come to understand is that once I've said my truth, I don't need to fight with others until they believe what I believe. I simply have to stand my ground.

Made in the USA
Middletown, DE
28 July 2017